The 5-Minute BIBLE STUDY for Men

ISBN 979-8-89151-139-2

Published by Barbour Publishing, Inc., 1810 Barbour Drive, Uhrichsville, Ohio 44683, www.barbourbooks.com

Our mission is to inspire the world with the life-changing message of the Bible.

Printed in the United States of America.

Paul Kent

The 5-Minute BIBLE STUDY for Men

Standing for God's Truth

INTRODUCTION

Do you ever find it hard to make time for Bible study? If so, you're not alone. Many of us intend to spend time in God's Word. . .but life just gets in the way. Before we know it, another week has passed and we've barely picked up our Bibles.

And yet we all know how important scripture is to our lives. We recognize it as the actual Word of God, the record of what He decided that human beings must know about Him and ourselves, about sin and salvation, about life and death and everything in between. We realize that God's truth is the only thing that can possibly change this dark world. We sense that we need to stand for God's truth in a culture that's increasingly hostile to it. But everything starts with truly understanding His Word.

That's why we created the 5-Minute Bible Study series. It provides an avenue for you to open the Bible each day and dig into an important passage, offering great benefit in just a few moments. Here's how the system works:

- Minutes 1–2: ***Read*** carefully the scripture passage for the day's Bible study.
- Minute 3: ***Understand***. Ponder a couple of prompts designed to help you apply the

verses to your own life. Consider these throughout your day as well.

- Minute 4: ***Apply***. Read a devotion based on the day's scriptural focus.
- Minute 5: ***Pray***. A prayer starter will help you to begin a time of conversation with God. Remember to allow time for Him to speak into your life as well.

There are ninety-three studies in this book, covering the essential topics of God's Word, God Himself, the human condition, Jesus, salvation, the Holy Spirit, self-denial, prayer, the world, spiritual warfare, and your eternal reward as a committed follower of Christ.

May *The 5-Minute Bible Study for Men: Standing for God's Truth* help you to establish the discipline of studying God's Word. Find a quiet place in your home, head out to your favorite coffee shop, or sit alone in your vehicle with this book and your Bible. Your willingness to spend five minutes focused on God's Word and prayer can make a huge difference in your day. . .and your entire life.

STANDING ON GOD'S TRUTH

READ MATTHEW 7:24–29

Key Verse:

"Everyone who hears these words of mine and puts them into practice is like a wise man who built his house on the rock."
MATTHEW 7:24 NIV

Understand:

- How much of your personal belief system is based specifically on God's Word?
- What other influences contribute to your worldview? What are the positives and negatives of each?

Apply:

Did you notice anything unusual about the title of today's study? It differs slightly from the title of this book. The variance is intentional—you can't stand *for* God's truth until you stand *on* it.

Today's scripture passage concludes Jesus' famed Sermon on the Mount. Matthew 5–7 contains His teaching on topics such as blessedness (5:3–12); Christians as salt and light in the world

(5:13–16); anger, adultery, and divorce (5:21–32); and love for one's enemies (5:43–48). Jesus gave insights on praying (6:5–15), storing up treasure in heaven (6:19–24), and worrying (6:25–34). He laid out the dangers of hypocrisy and judging (7:1–6), the rewards for persistent prayer (7:7–12), and the consequences of false faith (7:15–23). And He finished His teaching with a parable of wise and foolish builders: Everyone who listens to His words—and lives accordingly—is like a man who builds his house on a foundation of solid rock.

That type of house can weather the storms of life. Winds of fear and floods of opposition can't knock it down. The guy who lives there will be safe and secure because his base is solid.

Throughout the next three months, we'll consider numerous scriptures that you'll want to apply to your own life. As you do, you'll find yourself standing both *on* and *for* God's truth.

Pray:

Heavenly Father, help me to stand strong in this crazy world, building my life on the solid foundation of Your Word so I can weather every physical, emotional, and spiritual storm.

WHAT LASTS FOREVER?

READ ISAIAH 40:1–10

Key Verse:

"The grass withers and the flowers fade,
but the word of our God stands forever."
ISAIAH 40:8 NLT

Understand:

- What are the oldest physical items you own? How has time affected them?
- How have you witnessed the "fading" of other things—from personal relationships to societal values?

Apply:

The title of an old James Bond film says, "Diamonds Are Forever." But according to scripture, a day is coming when "the heavens will pass away with a terrible noise, and the very elements themselves will disappear in fire" (2 Peter 3:10 NLT). Not even diamonds will survive that fearsome "day of God" (verse 12 NLT).

This future of our sin-cursed earth is also the beginning of a purified, remade world where those who followed God by faith will live in perfection. We anticipate that day because of what He's said—His truthful Word that "stands forever."

As the timeless Maker of time, the limitless Creator of everything, God has the power and authority to make sweeping statements like the one in today's key verse. We all know that grass and flowers fade quickly, but even the Grand Canyon is wearing away, little by little, day by day. God's Word, though, is indestructible—because it is the outgrowth of His holy and all-powerful nature. God communicates Himself by His Word in ways that we finite human beings can understand. And if we live our lives as He demands, we'll enjoy His awesome, loving presence forever.

Isaiah 40 is a prophecy of Jesus, through whom we gain access to this amazing God. We can know Him as Creator, sustainer, Redeemer, and friend. And we can do all these things because of His amazing Word.

Pray:

I'm grateful that Your Word is as eternal as You are, Lord. And I thank You for giving Your Word as a guide for life. May I apply myself today to its incredible wisdom.

ORIGIN OF GOD'S WORD

READ EZEKIEL 1:1–28

Key Verse:

The word of the L*ORD came expressly to Ezekiel the priest, the son of Buzi, in the land of the Chaldeans by the river Chebar.*
EZEKIEL 1:3 SKJV

Understand:

- How much have you considered where your Bible comes from? What is your confidence level in God's Word?
- How do your answers to those questions affect your Christian walk?

Apply:

The fictional detective Sherlock Holmes was famed for his attention to detail. By carefully observing people's clothing, for example, he could quickly deduce their personal habits or recent whereabouts. As Christian men, let's take the same pains in our Bible reading.

Scripture wastes no words—every detail is important. Consider the term in today's key verse that describes how "the word of the LORD" came to Ezekiel: *expressly*. That indicates God specifically chose Ezekiel to receive the message. And it means the message was explicit—not vague or ambiguous.

Other writers had similar experiences: "the word of the LORD that came to Hosea" (1:1); "the word of the LORD that came to Joel" (1:1); "the word of the LORD that came to Micah" (1:1, all quotations SKJV).

God knew exactly what He wanted to communicate to human beings. He spoke very directly to the men He chose as Bible writers. They wrote in their own words and style, but only as they were "moved by the Holy Spirit" (2 Peter 1:21 SKJV).

We can be confident in what we read because it originated with God Himself. No human being dreamed up scripture. No man chose to "develop his ministry" by creating his own "Bible truth." The word of the Lord came expressly to the men He handpicked to write it down. Then God protected that truth through time so you can study with confidence today.

Pray:

Increase my knowledge of and confidence in Your Word, Lord. I know that it's vital to my life.

COMPLETELY RELIABLE

READ 2 PETER 1:12–21

Key Verse:

We also have the prophetic message as something completely reliable, and you will do well to pay attention to it, as to a light shining in a dark place, until the day dawns and the morning star rises in your hearts.

2 PETER 1:19 NIV

Understand:

- What distinguishes scripture from "cleverly devised stories" (2 Peter 1:16 NIV)? How can you know the difference?
- How is God's truth like "a light shining in a dark place" (verse 19 NIV)? When have you experienced that for yourself?

Apply:

If you're choosing something to build your life on, it ought to be completely reliable. That's how Peter described God's truth, the "prophetic message" we find in scripture.

Peter described himself as an eyewitness of Jesus' majesty. As the first of the apostles—both in order of his calling and in prominence among the twelve—he personally experienced all the amazing aspects of the Lord's ministry on earth. Peter shared this truth verbally and in writing, making "every effort," he said, "to see that after my departure you will always be able to remember these things" (2 Peter 1:15 NIV). He had the privilege of seeing Jesus' ministry; we have the privilege of learning from Peter's firsthand reporting. And firsthand, eyewitness testimony is always the most reliable.

In the case of scripture, it's more than "the most reliable"—it's absolutely, completely, and utterly reliable thanks to the Holy Spirit's involvement. As Peter said, "no prophecy of Scripture came about by the prophet's own interpretation of things" (2 Peter 1:20 NIV). He and his fellow Bible writers "spoke from God as they were carried along by the Holy Spirit" (verse 21 NIV).

This is truth you can trust—a foundation on which to build your entire life.

Pray:

Lord, I'm thankful that Your truth is completely reliable. Guide me as I read and study Your Word, and help me to stand both on and for it.

INSPIRED TRUTH

Read 2 Timothy 3:1–17

Key Verses:

All scripture is given by inspiration of God and is profitable for doctrine, for reproof, for correction, for instruction in righteousness, that the man of God may be perfect, thoroughly furnished for all good works.
2 Timothy 3:16–17 SKJV

Understand:

- How closely do the bad behaviors of verses 1 through 5 reflect what you see in modern society? Do any of them *not* apply?
- How do the final two verses of this chapter relate to the first nine?

Apply:

To say a work of art is "inspired" is to credit its brilliance, to a degree suggesting divine involvement. God's Word is certainly beautiful and moving, but it's much more than any song or painting or sculpture—and God's involvement was total. Though He used the talents of certain men to capture His Word for future generations, God actually "breathed out" the Bible text. That's the literal meaning of the word *inspiration* in today's key verses.

This understanding should supercharge our confidence in the truth of the Bible. If by faith we can believe in an all-powerful God who created all things, we can also trust that He would find a perfect way to communicate Himself to us. We can accept His inspiration—His breathing out—of the original Bible manuscripts. And we can believe that He protected His message of truth through the centuries as those manuscripts were kept and copied and ultimately translated into the Bible we carry today.

God put the physical breath of life into human beings (Genesis 2:7). And He put His spiritual breath into scripture, which provides everything we need to acquire salvation. "For the commandment is a lamp, and the law is light, and rebukes of instruction are the way of life" (Proverbs 6:23 SKJV).

Pray:

Lord, You clearly inspired Your Word. Now inspire me to read, study, and memorize it. Inspire me to stand for Your truth.

THE POWER OF GOD'S TRUTH

READ JEREMIAH 23:25–32

Key Verse:

"Is not my word like fire," declares the LORD,
"and like a hammer that breaks a rock in pieces?"
JEREMIAH 23:29 NIV

Understand:

- How much energy have you put into knowing God's Word? How well can you identify false teaching?
- In what ways is God's Word powerful? When have you seen God's truth change lives?

Apply:

Are you concerned about your culture? Do you fear the decline of morality, not only in your fellow citizens but among your leadership? Do you think many of your nation's religious leaders have lost their way? If so, welcome to Jeremiah's world.

The last great prophet of Judah, Jeremiah watched as the powerful Babylonians overthrew his beloved nation. That was God's punishment for His people's sin—the disobedience of princes, priests, and everyday people. For forty years, Jeremiah had warned them, trying to call them back to God. Sadly, they continued on their destructive way.

So was God's Word really that powerful? Was it truly like a fire or a hammer that breaks rock in pieces?

Yes. Whatever scripture says is true, simply because of its source. But think of it this way: Fire can be devastating, a conflagration that burns miles of grassland or forest. But immense fires begin as a single spark. Hammers certainly shatter rock, but only when wielded by a powerful arm. At other times, hammers simply lie quietly, awaiting their true work.

God's Word was powerful even in Jeremiah's day, changing individual lives. But in a few centuries, it changed the world, as the Roman empire embraced Christianity. Centuries after that, the West would also embrace scriptural principles and become the freest, most prosperous society in history.

Even as our culture grows spiritually cold and dark, God's Word is as powerful as ever—just waiting for Him to strike the match.

Pray:

Lord, please unleash the power of Your truth—in my life and in my world.

TWO-EDGED SWORD

Read Hebrews 4:1–13

Key Verse:

The word of God is alive and powerful. It is sharper than the sharpest two-edged sword, cutting between soul and spirit, between joint and marrow. It exposes our innermost thoughts and desires.
Hebrews 4:12 NLT

Understand:

- How is God's Word "alive"? What power does scripture hold?
- Why does the Bible identify itself as a "two-edged sword"? When have you felt its cutting?

Apply:

Today's key verse probably isn't new to you. It's one of the Bible's most familiar self-descriptions. But have you ever considered its context?

Hebrews 4 explains the "rest" God offers—peace in this world and the perfection of heaven to come. But this rest is available only if people have "listened to God" (verse 2 NLT). "Only we who believe can enter his rest," verse 3 continues. "As for the others, God said, 'In my anger I took an oath: "They will never enter my place of rest"'" (NLT).

This is God's all-encompassing truth, a positive invitation to follow Jesus by faith and a negative warning toward those who won't. While some spiritual truths can be deduced from nature—for example, God's wisdom and power in creating the universe—specific truths of salvation must be laid out in His Word. And Hebrews 4:12 clearly explains the power of that Word.

The Bible actually gives life. It's not some dry reference work, providing an occasional nugget of trivia. Nor is it a popular novel, to be read today and forgotten next week. No—scripture is God's Word, and it pierces our hearts with His truth. It's a double-edged sword, cutting in every direction. . .knocking out both our pride and our feelings of worthlessness. It cuts one way with rebuke and the other with hope.

When you stand both on and for this truth, you receive the rest God promised—both now and forever.

Pray:

May Your Word completely renew my thoughts and desires, Lord.

SCRIPTURE MUST BE FULFILLED

READ ACTS 1:15–26

Key Verse:

"Men and brothers, this scripture needed to have been fulfilled, which the Holy Spirit spoke before by the mouth of David concerning Judas, who was a guide to those who took Jesus."
ACTS 1:16 SKJV

Understand:

- What was the "scripture" that Peter referred to in this passage? What weight did Peter give to that scripture?
- What were the qualifications of an apostle, according to verses 21 and 22? How can this strengthen your confidence in what you know about Jesus Christ?

Apply:

Judas Iscariot's treachery did not surprise God. Jesus wasn't shocked by the betrayal of one of His twelve disciples. In ways that are mysterious to us but completely within His omniscience (what we might call His "all-knowingness"), the Lord had always expected what would transpire with Jesus' arrest in Gethsemane. In fact, His Spirit had addressed the situation a thousand years earlier in the Psalms.

In the weeks between Jesus' resurrection and the Holy Spirit's arrival at Pentecost, when the number of Christians was only around 120, the apostle Peter called for a new apostle to replace Judas. After handing Jesus over to His enemies, Judas—crushed by remorse—had hanged himself. Recognizing prophecies of this situation in Psalms 69:25 and 109:8, which indicated that Judas would be completely lost and replaced by a better man, Peter declared these scriptures "needed to have been fulfilled." So he oversaw a process that culminated in a man named Matthias being named the twelfth apostle.

Peter was standing for God's truth. This leader of the apostles made sure that he played a part in whatever God's Word called for. Today, we as Christians have that same privilege and responsibility. Let's study the scriptures carefully and, in God's power, do whatever they say.

Pray:

Lord God, what scriptures can I help to fulfill today? Give me Your wisdom, guidance, and courage to do exactly as You direct.

"YA GOTTA BELIEVE"

READ ROMANS 4:16–25

Key Verses:

The words "it was credited to him" were written not for him alone, but also for us, to whom God will credit righteousness—for us who believe in him who raised Jesus our Lord from the dead.

ROMANS 4:23–24 NIV

Understand:

- What does it mean to be "credited" righteousness?
- Who does the crediting? How is this righteousness gained?

Apply:

Serious baseball fans may recognize the title of today's study as the rallying cry of the 1973 Mets. In the National League East, New York won 19 of 26 games beginning in August, clinching the division on the final day. "Ya gotta believe," brainchild of reliever Tug McGraw, carried the Mets through a League Championship Series against Cincinnati and into Game 7 of the World Series with Oakland. But it couldn't quite propel New York to the title.

Believing in yourself only goes so far. Biblically speaking, "ya gotta believe" in Jesus.

The Old Testament clearly states that Abraham's belief in God is what made him righteous in the Lord's sight (Genesis 15:6). As today's key verses show, the New Testament reaffirms that reality for all who trust in God by believing in Jesus' death, burial, and resurrection. He died on a cross to take the punishment for human sin; He was buried to confirm His death; and He was raised again to show His power over sin and Satan. Taken together, this is the truth of the gospel that saves our souls (1 Corinthians 15:3–4).

When we stand *on* this truth, we're confirmed in our faith and receive assurance of heaven to come. And as we stand *for* this truth, we point others to the eternal life we ourselves have found.

Pray:

I'm grateful, Lord, that salvation is so simple—I don't have to pay for it or work to deserve it; I just believe in You. Help me share this remarkable truth with others.

BENEFITS OF TRUTH

READ JOHN 20:24–31

Key Verse:

These are written that you may believe that Jesus is the Messiah, the Son of God, and that by believing you may have life in his name.
JOHN 20:31 NIV

Understand:

- What important events occurred earlier in this chapter?
- According to Jesus Himself, what makes a person "blessed" or "happy" (verse 29)? How many Christians through time have fallen into this category?

Apply:

Christians of all stripes recognize the first entry in the Westminster Shorter Catechism, a seventeenth-century teaching tool created by English and Scottish believers: "Question: What is the chief end of man? Answer: Man's chief end is to glorify God, and to enjoy Him forever."

In just twelve words, that answer summarizes the entire message of scripture. God, who alone created the universe and sets the standard of holiness, saves people primarily for His own glory. But when we follow Him by faith in Christ, we benefit—we "enjoy Him forever."

That was the apostle John's point in today's key verse. By believing that Jesus is the Messiah, the Savior who died for our sins and rose again, we gain life—life that's eternal (John 3:16) and full (John 10:10). These are benefits of giving ourselves fully to God's truth.

Jesus' disciple Thomas struggled to believe that his Lord had overcome the gruesome crucifixion. Thomas needed physical confirmation of the resurrection, which he was given. But Jesus told Thomas that those who could believe purely by faith—and that includes all of us—are blessed. We are happy when we simply trust in a glorious God who allows us to enjoy His presence. The Holy Spirit inside us guarantees our eternal life (which has already begun) and makes it full as we yield to His leading. What greater benefit could we desire?

Pray:

Thank You, Lord, for blessing me with full, eternal life. May I show my gratitude by bringing glory to Your name.

THE ULTIMATE TRUTH

READ GENESIS 1:1–31

Key Verse:

In the beginning God created the heaven and the earth.
GENESIS 1:1 SKJV

Understand:

- How easy or hard is it for you to accept the idea of an eternal, self-existent, all-powerful God? Why?
- What other explanations are there for the existence of the universe? How compelling do you find them to be?

Apply:

Christians of good will may differ on the when's and how's and why's of creation, but we should all agree on this basic idea: Our universe and everything in it originated with God. He predates space and time and caused all physical things to exist. His life breathed life into our world. His mental abilities are what power human thinking, including our ability to discern truth.

Truth is whatever aligns with reality. We who already know and follow Jesus Christ accept the reality of scripture, which describes this infinite God and what He's done in creation. But even people who don't yet know Christ can see God's fingerprints all over the universe. The apostle Paul elaborated on this in Romans 1:18–20.

Throughout history, many people have tried to write God out of the story, to find other ways to explain reality. Often, this has been an attempt to avoid accountability to God, whose perfect goodness is legitimately frightening to broken human beings. But there is a further truth at play, that this holy God is also generous and loving. He will gladly adopt anyone who comes to Him by humble faith in His Son, Jesus.

"Truth" covers every aspect of the universe, from the behavior of light to the law of gravity to the basics of human chromosomes. Everything that is real derives from the ultimate truth, God Himself. We do well to ensure that our beliefs agree with whatever He's said.

Pray:

Lord God, the vastness of the universe and the intricacy of the human body both point to an incredible Creator—they point to You. May I always align my beliefs with this ultimate truth.

IF GOD IS REAL. . .

READ EXODUS 20:1–11

Key Verses:

"You must not have any other god but me. You must not make for yourself an idol of any kind or an image of anything in the heavens or on the earth or in the sea. You must not bow down to them or worship them, for I, the LORD your God, am a jealous God who will not tolerate your affection for any other gods."
EXODUS 20:3–5 NLT

Understand:

- What false gods are actually promoted as gods? What other things do we make false gods by our attitudes?
- What false god poses the most danger to you? Why?

Apply:

Exodus 20 records the Ten Commandments, the foundational laws God gave to Israel. Just weeks after breaking them free of their Egyptian slavery, God provided overarching rules for their behavior as His people. He began by demanding their complete loyalty.

Israelites were to have no (lowercase) gods and were expressly forbidden any physical idols or images. Their worship belonged solely to the true (capital *G*) God. As Jesus explained centuries later, "God is Spirit, so those who worship him must worship in spirit and in truth" (John 4:24 NLT). Deviation from God's standard would provoke Him to jealousy.

Perhaps we wince when God calls Himself "jealous." After all, isn't that pretty much the same as *envy*? The two terms are close in meaning. . .but have an important difference. Envy is a desire for another's stuff, while jealousy is a protective attitude toward one's own possessions—in God's case, His honor, glory, and good name.

We fault a man when he envies another for his wife, but we commend one who is jealous of his own. In God's case, if He is who He claims to be, He has every right to demand our attention and worship. God is God—and we benefit when we acknowledge and obey Him.

Pray:

Lord, I admit that You are the true God. You alone are worthy of worship.

ETERNAL GOD, ETERNAL TRUTH

Read Isaiah 43:1–13

Key Verses:

"You are my witnesses," declares the Lord, *"and my servant whom I have chosen, so that you may know and believe me and understand that I am he. Before me no god was formed, nor will there be one after me. I, even I, am the* Lord, *and apart from me there is no savior."*
Isaiah 43:10–11 NIV

Understand:

- How would you define *eternal*? How easy or hard is it to comprehend the concept of eternity?
- How might God's eternality and His omnipotence (all-powerfulness) relate? Why?

Apply:

The prophet Isaiah spoke specifically to the ancient nation of Israel, but with principles that apply to us. As the seventeenth-century Bible commentator Matthew Henry put it, Isaiah was "looking at the release of the Jews out of their captivity, but looking through that, and beyond that, to the great work of man's redemption by Jesus Christ, and the grace of the gospel, which through Him believers partake of."

God promised to use His power for His people's benefit, regathering the Israelites from the nations to which they'd been scattered. Sometimes He would use powerful pagan leaders for His own purposes (see Isaiah 41:2–3). No false god could accomplish anything like this (Isaiah 43:9). God—the one true God—could perfectly predict and fulfill such things because of His omnipotence, an outgrowth of His eternality.

The God of infinite existence must have equally infinite power. As He said through Isaiah, "'I have revealed and saved and proclaimed—I, and not some foreign god among you. You are my witnesses,' declares the LORD, 'that I am God. Yes, and from ancient days I am he. No one can deliver out of my hand. When I act, who can reverse it?'" (43:12–13 NIV).

Pray:

Lord, You are just as truthful as You are strong and eternal. Help me to believe everything You say.

YOU ARE NOT GOD

READ JOB 40:6–14

Key Verse:

"Do you have an arm like God's,
and can your voice thunder like his?"
JOB 40:9 NIV

Understand:

- How do we as human beings sometimes try to usurp God's role and authority?
- When has God shown you that you are not in ultimate control of your life? What was that realization like?

Apply:

The title of today's study seems obvious, but it's human nature to think of ourselves in God's place—as self-contained, self-sustaining beings who make our own rules. That's part of the pride that underlies our sin nature.

Today's key verse shatters those illusions. In it, God Himself speaks to Job—a man who, according to scripture, was "blameless and upright" and who "feared God and shunned evil" (Job 1:1 NIV). Job suffered almost unimaginable losses at the hands of Satan. . .by permission of God. In fact, the Lord had actually directed Satan's attention to Job: "Have you considered my servant Job? There is no one on earth like him" (Job 1:8 NIV).

Even after his wealth, his children, and his own health were destroyed, "Job did not sin by charging God with wrongdoing" (Job 1:22 NIV). But over time, Job's frustration began to boil over, bringing him closer and closer to that red line. At one point, he complained, "I cry out to you, God, but you do not answer; I stand up, but you merely look at me. You turn on me ruthlessly; with the might of your hand you attack me" (Job 30:20–21 NIV).

God defended Himself by posing a series of questions to Job, questions like those of Job 40:9. They all led to the obvious conclusion: Job was not God.

Neither are we. This is a foundational truth by which to live our lives.

Pray:

Lord God, forgive me for the times I try to usurp Your authority. Tame my pride for Your glory.

GOD IS BEYOND

READ ACTS 17:16–31

Key Verses:

"He is the God who made the world and everything in it. Since he is Lord of heaven and earth, he doesn't live in man-made temples, and human hands can't serve his needs—for he has no needs. He himself gives life and breath to everything, and he satisfies every need."
ACTS 17:24–25 NLT

Understand:

- How do the attitudes and philosophies of Athens in Paul's day resemble those of our time? How do they differ?
- What sets God apart from any other deity or belief system?

Apply:

When the apostle Paul visited Athens in the decades after Jesus' death and resurrection, he undoubtedly saw the Parthenon, the many-columned temple of Athena, overlooking the city. This massive shrine was hardly the only evidence of false gods in Athens. Scripture says Paul was "deeply troubled by all the idols he saw everywhere" (Acts 17:16 NLT).

Athena was the Greeks' god of wisdom and warfare. Other gods supposedly oversaw the sun, the sea, agriculture, and many other aspects of the world. In his missionary zeal, Paul wanted to correct the Athenians' error. But he did so with tact, referencing a shrine he'd seen that was dedicated "To an Unknown God." "This God, whom you worship without knowing," Paul explained, "is the one I'm telling you about" (Acts 17:23 NLT).

The true God, unknown to the people of Athens, was beyond any other so-called god they followed. He made everything, governs everything, and exists complete in and of Himself. God doesn't need anything from anyone, though He does want people to know Him (verse 27). That's possible through Jesus, God in human flesh, who died and rose again to prove His power (verses 30–31).

Standing for God's truth means standing in the truth of God—beginning with His absolute supremacy over all things.

Pray:

Give me glimpses of Your "beyondness," Lord. Don't let my focus stray to lesser things.

INCREDIBLE OR NOT?

Read Acts 26:1–18

Key Verse:

"Why should any of you consider it incredible that God raises the dead?"
Acts 26:8 NIV

Understand:

- How easy or hard is it for you to believe the miracles of the Bible? Why?
- What does the resurrection of Jesus mean to the Christian faith? To your own faith?

Apply:

Thomas Jefferson, third president of the United States, created a personal version of the New Testament. It retained Jesus' moral teachings but dispensed with His miracles—from turning water into wine to His resurrection from the dead.

The Bible's supernatural events have been, and continue to be, a stumbling block to many. Jesus walking on water? Feeding five thousand men with a young boy's lunch? Calming a storm with a simple command? *Come on!*

All of these miracles turn the laws of nature on their heads. But why do "laws of nature" even exist? How is it that we live in an orderly universe governed by consistent rules that prevent water walking or the multiplying of loaves and fishes or dead people returning to life?

The apostle Paul, on trial before Roman officials and the Rome-approved "king" over Jerusalem, declared that he had "conformed to the strictest sect of our [Jewish] religion, living as a Pharisee" (Acts 26:5 NIV). That group revered Moses and the scriptures he wrote, including the declaration "In the beginning God created the heavens and the earth" (Genesis 1:1 NIV). If He could do that simply by speaking, "Why should any of you consider it incredible that God raises the dead?"

As humans, we can't fathom the power that created this entire universe *ex nihilo*—from nothing. But as Christians, we take this truth by faith, living in awe of the God who can and did. All other miracles simply fall into place.

Pray:

Lord God, everything You do is incredible to the human mind—yet perfectly in line with Your infinite power and wisdom.

GOD IS THE ULTIMATE SOURCE

READ 1 CHRONICLES 29:1–19

Key Verse:

"But who am I, and who are my people,
that we could give anything to you?
Everything we have has come from you,
and we give you only what you first gave us!"
1 CHRONICLES 29:14 NLT

Understand:

- Why is the phrase "self-made man" misleading?
- What do human beings need in order to create things? What did God need?

Apply:

The "self-made man" is one who rises from humble circumstances to attain great heights of wealth, power, or fame. In American political history, self-made men include Benjamin Franklin, Abraham Lincoln, and Ronald Reagan. In business, oil magnate John D. Rockefeller, McDonald's founder Ray Kroc, and Walmart patriarch Sam Walton. In other realms, inventor Thomas Edison, social reformer Frederick Douglass, and Supreme Court Justice Clarence Thomas.

But in spite of their obvious hard, smart work, none of these men were "self-made" at the most basic level. *God* made them and gave them the personality and skills they then used to achieve remarkable things.

None of us made our own bodies. None of us provided our first breath—or the millions of breaths since then. None of us build anything except from the raw materials that God Himself provided.

This was King David's point as he thanked God for the gold, silver, wood, and other materials he gathered for Solomon to build the temple in Jerusalem. And this is a truth we as followers of Christ must understand and live by. In our faith journey, there is no allowance for human pride—in fact, God despises it and promises to humble those who exalt themselves (Matthew 23:12).

We are, in reality, utterly dependent on God for everything. As we acknowledge this truth, we honor God. And honoring God is always good for us.

Pray:

Lord, thank You for providing everything in my life—without You, I have and am nothing. Keep me humble before You.

GOD POWERS YOUR GOOD WORKS

READ 2 CORINTHIANS 9:6–13

Key Verse:

God is able to bless you abundantly,
so that in all things at all times,
having all that you need, you will
abound in every good work.
2 CORINTHIANS 9:8 NIV

Understand:

- Why would God do many of His good works through His children?
- When have you "abounded" in a good work? What was that like?

Apply:

We get much of our theology—especially our understanding of sin and salvation—from the apostle Paul's letters. But look closely at them and you'll also get an interesting glimpse of everyday Christian service: the ongoing storyline of a collection for poor believers around Jerusalem.

The exact reason for the need is unclear. Some speculate that Judea was suffering famine; others suggest that the persecuted Christians were being locked out of the Jewish economy. Whatever the case, Paul urged Gentile believers in Romans 15, 1 Corinthians 16, and 2 Corinthians 8–9 to contribute to their Jewish brothers' needs.

"Good works" are encouraged throughout the New Testament, though never as the means of salvation. The good we do for others is an outgrowth of the good God does for us in salvation. That is not to say unbelievers don't perform good deeds—the image of God is still reflected in every person. But when we accept God's free gift of salvation by faith in Christ, He gives us the will, the strength, and the resources to "abound in every good work."

Christians stand on the truth of shared compassion, received from God and passed along to others. We are His tools for meeting others' needs, inside and outside the church. Therefore, we must never boast of our good works. . .but should rather say, like the servants Jesus described, "we have only done our duty" (Luke 17:10 NIV).

Pray:

Lord, please show me the good You want me to accomplish today—then empower my obedience.

YOU ARE PROTECTED BY GOD

Read Jude 17–25

Key Verse:

Now all glory to God, who is able to keep you from falling away and will bring you with great joy into his glorious presence without a single fault.
Jude 24 NLT

Understand:

- How can Christians "build each other up in [their] most holy faith" (Jude 20 NLT)?
- What is your responsibility in your Christian life? What is God's?

Apply:

Many people, sometimes even true Christians, confuse our human responsibilities before God. To be saved, we don't perform a single work—we simply believe in the work Jesus did on the cross. To grow in faith, we *must* work—and that's a tough, lifelong process. To successfully reach heaven, we trust entirely in God's protective care—He will, as Jude says, "keep you from falling away and will bring you with great joy into his glorious presence without a single fault."

If heaven-bound Christians are kept from falling away, other people apparently do fall away on their journey. But biblically speaking, their faith wasn't real—or else God would have kept them. Consider Jesus' parable of the soils, in which different kinds of people seemingly accept the "seed" of the gospel message. . .but only one type of person actually shows life by producing fruit (Matthew 13:1–23).

To understand exactly how and why God chooses some people for salvation is far above our pay grade. Nor can we grasp why true Christians vary so widely in their spiritual growth. But if we do as Paul urged—examine ourselves and find that our faith is genuine (2 Corinthians 13:5)—then we can trust that God will see us through this life and into His eternal presence.

By standing both on and for this truth, we honor God's goodness and mercy. We glorify Him for protecting His own.

Pray:

Lord, please confirm my faith and give me unbreakable confidence in Your eternal protection.

OUR TRUE HUMAN CONDITION

READ GENESIS 3:1–19

Key Verse:

And he said, "Who told you that you were naked? Have you eaten from the tree that I commanded you not to eat from?"
GENESIS 3:11 NIV

Understand:

- Why do you think God allowed the free will that brought sin into His good creation?
- How does Adam and Eve's sin so long ago still affect us today?

Apply:

Sin is a pandemic with a 100 percent fatality rate. Patient zero was the very first human being, who chose to disobey God's one negative command: Don't eat from the tree of the knowledge of good and evil. By doing that anyway, Adam, along with his wife, Eve, got a lot more knowledge than they bargained for. Suddenly, they knew all about guilt, shame, and separation from their Creator.

Why would God permit this first couple to choose something that would ruin His "very good" (Genesis 1:31) creation? Somehow, for His own wise purposes, God allowed rebellion against His absolute sovereignty, and the resulting curse He pronounced has affected every human being since—present company included. The divine punishment of thorns and thistles, hard work and death has been (and continues to be) inescapable. No one is exempt from the ravages of sin, because we all participate in it: "There is no one on earth who is righteous, no one who does what is right and never sins" (Ecclesiastes 7:20 NIV).

This is our true condition, and we are wise to admit it. We human beings are not basically good, nor are we capable of perfecting ourselves. Deep down, we are all rebels against our perfect Creator, deeply in need of the help that only He can provide. Happily for us, He is able and willing—eager, even—to save all who humbly turn to Him.

Pray:

Lord, I acknowledge my rebellion against You and ask for Your help to completely renounce it.

EVIL ALL THE TIME

READ GENESIS 6:1–8

Key Verse:

The LORD saw how great the wickedness of the human race had become on the earth, and that every inclination of the thoughts of the human heart was only evil all the time.
GENESIS 6:5 NIV

Understand:

- How could human sin become so bad so quickly after Adam and Eve's disobedience?
- What does scripture mean when it says, "Every inclination of the thoughts of the human heart was only evil all the time"?

Apply:

Exactly who the Nephilim of Genesis 6 were is beyond the scope of our study. Suffice it to say that they were involved in a whirl of human sin that grieved God so badly He decided to push the world's reset button.

By just the tenth generation after Adam, wickedness was "great" on earth. The omniscient God could read the completely evil inclinations of every human mind. There was no relief from the sin that washed over people's lives like ocean waves. . .except within the righteous Noah and his family.

Besides him, his wife, and their three sons and their wives, humanity was a lost cause. Not even the image of God within people was enough to save them from their evil ways. God decided to wipe everything away with a gigantic flood.

This is the danger of sin—a danger we see exploding like a mushroom cloud in our own time. Our culture is declining fast, and we must be careful not to be dragged down with it.

Happily for us, we Christians have a benefit that not even Noah enjoyed: the permanent presence of God's Holy Spirit in our lives. This "Spirit of truth" (John 16:13) guides us into all truth. . .including the foundational reality that, apart from God, we are "evil all the time."

Pray:

Lord, it's humbling to think of myself as completely sinful. But that's the starting point for my spiritual healing.

NO ONE IS GOOD

Read Psalm 53:1–6

Key Verses:

God looks down from heaven on the entire human race; he looks to see if anyone is truly wise, if anyone seeks God. But no, all have turned away; all have become corrupt. No one does good, not a single one!
Psalm 53:2–3 NLT

Understand:

- What two groups of people does this psalm reference? What are their similarities and differences?
- Why does God put up with "fools"? What is His great desire for all people (see 2 Peter 3:9)?

Apply:

If you're reading straight through the Psalms—and you have a good memory—Psalm 53 will be familiar. It's an almost exact repeat of Psalm 14.

People have noted that when God says anything, we should pay attention. But if He repeats something, we'd be fools to ignore it.

Incidentally, "fools" are the first people we meet

in Psalms 14 and 53. They're the people who say in their hearts, "There is no God" (verse 1). And as God scans the entire earth, He finds that the rest of humanity doesn't fare much better—*all* are immoral.

The news, to this point, is bad. But by verse 4, we get a glimmer of hope: God has people of His own. They are included in the "no one does good" crowd, but He has chosen them anyway. And now, though far from perfect, these people can at least begin to honor and serve God—to be something more than "corrupt" and "evil" (verse 1). That was true of the Israelites when David wrote these psalms, and it's even more true today, after the life and work of Jesus. The moment we accept Jesus by faith, God actually gives us new birth.

We're still sinful human beings, but God considers us as perfect as His flawless Son. Goodness is credited to our account for our belief in Christ.

Pray:

I believe, Lord—thank You for applying Your goodness to me.

YOU CAN'T TRUST ANYONE. . .

READ MICAH 7:1–7

Key Verse:

The faithful have been swept from the land; not one upright person remains. Everyone lies in wait to shed blood; they hunt each other with nets.
MICAH 7:2 NIV

Understand:

- How was Micah's time similar to ours? Are there differences?
- How does God's Spirit in believers change things—individually and culturally?

Apply:

Old Testament prophets had a tough job. They spoke out for God and righteousness in a culture that cared little for either. In Micah's day—perhaps during the reign of Judah's wicked King Ahaz—the prophet lamented that he couldn't find a faithful person in the entire land.

Today's key verse is probably an exaggeration, either for effect or because Micah truly felt alone in his commitment. But remember that when another Old Testament prophet, Elijah, voiced similar feelings, God said, "I reserve seven thousand in Israel—all whose knees have not bowed down to Baal" (1 Kings 19:18 NIV).

Still, vast numbers of people today, even some who claim Christianity, are "skilled in doing evil" (Micah 7:3 NIV). And the prophet issued a warning: "Do not trust a neighbor; put no confidence in a friend. Even with the woman who lies in your embrace guard the words of your lips. For a son dishonors his father, a daughter rises up against her mother, a daughter-in-law against her mother-in-law—a man's enemies are the members of his own household" (verses 5–6 NIV).

Apart from the work of God in our own lives, we're all selfish, seeking our own interests. Even as born-again, Spirit-filled believers, we sometimes default to choices that elevate our own desires over the well-being of others.

Micah might add, "Don't even trust yourself."

Pray:

Lord, I know I'm capable of selfish, sinful choices. Fill me with Your goodness and protect me from myself.

GONE ASTRAY

READ ISAIAH 53:1–12

Key Verse:

We all like sheep have gone astray.
We have turned, each one, to his
own way, and the LORD has laid
on Him the iniquity of us all.
ISAIAH 53:6 SKJV

Understand:

- What does it mean to "go astray"? What are people straying from?
- Besides their tendency to wander, how else are people like sheep?

Apply:

According to *Merriam-Webster*, the term *sheeple*—an obvious mash-up of *sheep* and *people*—dates to 1945. But the idea goes back to Old Testament times. In Psalm 23, where "the Lord is my shepherd," David was the sheep. In today's key verse, Isaiah declared that "we all"—human beings—have gone astray like silly sheep. We wander off, away from the God who created, keeps, protects, and feeds us.

Sadly, this is the universal human condition:

weak and foolish, yet headstrong in straying. If it seems like people are bent on destroying themselves, they are—because of the sin we're all born into. Without help, we're doomed.

Help, though, is readily available. When Isaiah 53:6 speaks of someone on whom "the LORD has laid. . .the iniquity of us all," it's describing Jesus. This entire chapter is a messianic prophecy, a prediction of God's "anointed one"—the Messiah (from Hebrew) or Christ (from Greek). Though Jesus was still in the future for Isaiah, we know He lived and died and won our salvation two thousand years ago. Jesus took on Himself every human sin—every weak, foolish, and headstrong thing we've ever done—and covered it with His perfection. And now, as the good shepherd, He's seeking out lost sheep, calling them to Himself for provision and protection.

If you're already in His fold, stick close. If you're not, today would be the perfect time to heed His call.

Pray:

Thank You, Lord, for seeking me out when I strayed. When I feel that pull to wander away again, keep me close to Your side.

EVERYONE HAS SINNED . . .NO EXCEPTIONS

READ ROMANS 3:9–26

Key Verse:

For everyone has sinned; we all fall short of God's glorious standard.
ROMANS 3:23 NLT

Understand:

- Why is the Bible so insistent on the idea that "everyone has sinned" (see verses 9–18)?
- How is scripture's negativity toward people actually a sign of God's love?

Apply:

God's hatred of human pride is well documented throughout scripture. "You rebuke the arrogant," the psalmist wrote; "those who wander from your commands are cursed" (Psalm 119:21 NLT). "Haughty eyes" are one of seven things the Lord detests (see Proverbs 6:16–19). And God humbled prideful leaders like Pharaoh, Haman, and Nebuchadnezzar in very public ways.

On the other hand, humility pleases God and

helps us. "True humility and fear of the Lord," Proverbs 22:4 (NLT) says, "lead to riches, honor, and long life." Our salvation begins with humility, in fact, as we must admit our sinfulness and need of forgiveness before God can redeem our lives and put us on the road to heaven. That's why the Bible pulls no punches when it describes *all* people—each and every one of us—as sinful, falling short of God's "glorious standard."

Sinful pride tells us that we're not that bad. That's why many people, even some professing Christians, are uncomfortable with all this negativity. "Let's just focus on God's love," they say.

But if God is perfect (He is) and His standards are equally high (they are), then we need to admit that we don't measure up. It's only when we humbly acknowledge these truths that He can and will work in our lives. God is eager to save sinful people—but we accept the free gift of salvation on His terms, not our own.

Pray:

Thank You for telling me the truth Lord—on my own, I'm not good at all. Help me to humbly accept Your goodness in my life.

DON'T DECEIVE YOURSELF

Read 1 John 1:5–10

Key Verse:

If we claim to be without sin, we deceive ourselves and the truth is not in us.
1 John 1:8 NIV

Understand:

- What does this passage mean when it warns against claiming to be without sin?
- What harsh words and phrases does John use throughout this passage? Why?

Apply:

The good news of the gospel is that Jesus saves souls. The bad news is that souls *need* saving because they're warped by sin, rebellious against God. To emphasize the good news while downplaying the bad isn't helpful—in fact, it's dangerous.

To be truly saved, we must acknowledge our sin against God and accept the Lord's solution for that sin. But when we act like we haven't sinned, the process falls apart. God will only apply Jesus' blood to the person who knows he needs it. That's why in today's passage, John speaks strongly against any mindset that tries to raise people to God's level of "light"—the glory of His perfection—apart from "the blood of Jesus, his Son, [which] purifies us from all sin" (verse 7 NIV).

If we say we've never committed sin—or if we argue that the wrong things we do aren't actually sinful—John declares that we "deceive ourselves." If we're self-deceived, "the truth is not in us." If the truth is not in us, "we make [God] out to be a liar and his word is not in us" (verse 10). If God's Word is not in us, how can we possibly be born again?

This is the slippery slope of denying or redefining sin to make ourselves feel better. God's truth is that He is light and we are darkness. As long as we agree to His assessment, we have hope.

Pray:

Heavenly Father, I don't ever want to deceive myself in such important things. Give me the humility I need to admit my sin and appreciate the salvation You provide through Jesus.

HOPE FOR SINNERS

READ PSALM 130:1–8

Key Verse:

LORD, if you kept a record of our sins,
who, O Lord, could ever survive?
PSALM 130:3 NLT

Understand:

- How many ways are there to sin against God? How many sins would be on your record?
- According to this psalm, what hope do sinners have?

Apply:

Some people are worse sinners than others, but *everybody* sins. Israel's great king David, known as a man after God's own heart (1 Samuel 13:14; Acts 13:22), admitted, "I was born a sinner—yes, from the moment my mother conceived me" (Psalm 51:5 NLT). This was part of his confession of adultery and murder in the sad case of Bathsheba.

That was an appalling incident in David's life, and a stark warning to all of us of what can happen when we allow temptation to draw our eyes from God. And it's not just the "big sins" we should fear.

The Bible commands us to avoid gossip, dishonesty, complaining, and lust. . .and says if we fail in just one area, we're no better off than the person who breaks every law (James 2:10).

Happily for us, God doesn't *want* to keep records of sin. He prefers to forgive and forget: "You offer forgiveness, that we might learn to fear you. . . . With the Lord there is unfailing love. His redemption overflows" (Psalm 130:4, 7 NLT). In this age of grace, when we simply accept the gift of salvation through faith in Jesus, we enjoy the "new covenant" blessings God described through Jeremiah: "I will forgive their wickedness, and I will never again remember their sins" (31:34 NLT).

Don't ever think your sins aren't important. They're deadly serious—but so was God's solution. He sent Jesus to die on the cross for every wrong thing you've ever done. . .or will do.

Pray:

It's true, Lord—I'm a great sinner. But You are a greater forgiver. Thank You for redeeming me.

THE SUPREMACY OF JESUS

Read John 1:1–14

Key Verse:

In the beginning was the Word, and the Word was with God, and the Word was God.

John 1:1 SKJV

Understand:

- What important names or descriptions of Jesus are given in this passage? What do they indicate?
- How does Jesus compare with God the Father? How do they differ?

Apply:

It's okay to struggle with the concept of the Trinity, the idea that one God exists in three equal but distinct "persons"—Father, Son, and Spirit. Some things are just beyond our human comprehension. While many people find that frustrating, the reality is that a God who could be fully understood by our finite minds would be no God at all.

The Trinity is a truth we accept by faith, trusting the Bible's teaching even when we can't grasp its full depth. This introductory section of John's Gospel is clear about Jesus' deity—He was there with God "in the beginning" of creation, and He "was God." Jesus' name isn't mentioned through the first 16 verses of John 1, but He is plainly identified in verse 17. And the description of "the Word" becoming flesh and dwelling among us (verse 14) is an obvious reference to Jesus' life on earth.

As the Word, Jesus is God's understandable communication with human beings. And as the light (verses 6–9), Jesus allows us to see essential spiritual realities—the most important being the fact that we can "become the sons of God" (verse 12) by believing in His name.

As the second person of the Trinity, as the Creator of all things, as the Word of God and true light of humanity, as the glorious "only begotten of the Father" (verse 14), Jesus is absolutely supreme. If we wish to know God, we must know Jesus.

Pray:

Lord Jesus, thank You for making God understandable and attainable. Please help me to know You better every day.

GOD IN A BODY

READ COLOSSIANS 2:6–15

Key Verse:

In Christ all the fullness of the Deity lives in bodily form.
COLOSSIANS 2:9 NIV

Understand:

- Why would God, in Jesus, take on "bodily form"? What does that mean to us as human beings?
- What does "the fullness of the Deity" include?

Apply:

This passage of Colossians is rich in theology (the study and understanding of God), but we're focusing simply on verse 9.

While God the Father is an invisible spirit (John 1:18; Colossians 1:15; 1 Timothy 1:17; 1 John 4:12), Jesus was God in human flesh. While the third person of the Trinity—the Holy Spirit—is largely unseen (though He did appear in the form of a dove and as tongues of fire in the New Testament), Jesus was physically present on earth. People saw, heard, and even touched Him. Since "all the fullness of the Deity" was in Jesus' "bodily form," we as finite humans can better understand our infinite God.

Jesus is the glorious God, one with the Father and the Holy Spirit, but He "made himself nothing by taking the very nature of a servant, being made in human likeness" (Philippians 2:7 NIV). Why? "Since the children have flesh and blood, he too shared in their humanity so that by his death he might break the power of him who holds the power of death—that is, the devil" (Hebrews 2:14 NIV).

In His physical body, Jesus became the ultimate sacrifice for sin. Then, by physically rising from the dead, He proved His absolute power over death. To finish the thought from Hebrews, He would "free those who all their lives were held in slavery by their fear of death" (2:15 NIV).

The truth of the incarnation—Jesus' taking on a human body—is vital to your faith.

Pray:

Remind me, Lord, of the truth of Your incarnation. You were and are real—in fact, You're the ultimate reality.

VERY GOD OF VERY GOD

READ JOHN 10:22–33

Key Verse:

"The Father and I are one."
JOHN 10:30 NLT

Understand:

- How easy or difficult is it for you to accept the concept of the Trinity? Why?
- What do you think of the belief that Jesus is not divine? How does this passage contradict that idea?

Apply:

"Very God of very God" is a phrase from the Nicene Creed, a fourth-century statement of Christian belief. Church leaders convened in the city of Nicaea in AD 325 to address the ideas of a man named Arius, who claimed that Jesus was not actually God. Among other things, Arianism argued that Jesus' death on the cross proved that He was not the immortal Deity. The church council disagreed, however, crafting a creed that described Jesus as "the only-begotten Son of God, begotten of the Father before all worlds; God of God, Light of Light, very God of very God; begotten, not made, being of one substance with the Father."

Arguments over Jesus' deity have continued over the centuries, even though His own words in John 10 plainly describe oneness with the Father. And if for some reason this statement is unconvincing to modern readers, look at how Jesus' contemporaries understood it: They picked up stones to execute Him for blasphemy. "You, a mere man," they fumed, "claim to be God" (John 10:33 NLT).

Jesus' hateful opponents weren't able to grasp this truth because they didn't belong to Him—"You are not my sheep," He told them (John 10:26 NLT). We who are part of Jesus' flock know the truth, and His Godhood provides confidence and comfort. Since Jesus is God, we can be sure of our salvation. No one will ever snatch us from His—or the Father's—hand (verses 28–29).

Pray:

Lord Jesus, I'm so glad that You are God. My eternal future is secure in Your hands.

ONE IN GOD

READ JOHN 17:6–26

Key Verses:

"My prayer is not for them alone. I pray also for those who will believe in me through their message, that all of them may be one, Father, just as you are in me and I am in you. May they also be in us so that the world may believe that you have sent me."

JOHN 17:20–21 NIV

Understand:

- For what two groups of people does Jesus pray in this passage?
- What were Jesus' requests for each group?

Apply:

Mention "the Lord's Prayer," and most people will think of verses in Matthew 6 and Luke 11, where Jesus taught His disciples how to pray. But many have noted that John 17 is the actual Lord's Prayer, since it presents the most extensive record of things Jesus Himself asked of His Father in heaven. This chapter of John has come to be known as "the High Priestly Prayer."

And what was the high priest praying? That

His handpicked disciples would be protected from "the evil one" (John 17:15 NIV) and sanctified—that is, set apart—"by the truth; your word is truth" (verse 17 NIV).

Beyond His original disciples, though, Jesus prayed for all of us who follow Him today: "those who will believe in me through [the disciples'] message" (John 17:20 NIV). He asked His Father for every individual who accepts Him as Lord to be "one," "in us," and "brought to complete unity" (verses 21, 23 NIV). This will ultimately bring glory to God—a glory we will someday see in person (verses 22–24).

By His very nature, Jesus is one with God. And we are unified with God by knowing and accepting His truth, which we find in His unchanging Word.

Pray:

Lord Jesus, make me one with Yourself and my fellow believers. I want to glorify You and Your Father by my wholehearted acceptance of Your truth.

JESUS BECAME A MAN

READ 1 JOHN 4:1–6

Key Verse:

This is how we know if they have the Spirit of God: If a person claiming to be a prophet acknowledges that Jesus Christ came in a real body, that person has the Spirit of God.
1 JOHN 4:2 NLT

Understand:

- Why is it important for Jesus to have had a true human body?
- Why would someone deny Jesus' physical incarnation?

Apply:

The doctrine of the Trinity affirms Jesus' deity, that He was (and is and always will be) one with God the Father and the Holy Spirit. But the Bible's teaching on the Trinity clearly shows that the three persons of the Godhead are distinct. Jesus demonstrated His uniqueness by becoming a part of His own human creation.

When John wrote his New Testament letters, some self-proclaimed prophets were apparently questioning the incarnation. Theologians say that

Gnosticism, a heresy plaguing the early church, viewed the spirit as good and the body as evil. Perhaps some of the false teachers of John's day were trying to "protect" Jesus from any connection with the physical.

But though the Bible teaches that the physical world has been deeply marred by sin, it never describes physical things as inherently evil. And scripture is unambiguous when it says Jesus, the "Lamb of God" (John 1:29 NLT), was born into a real body, experienced life as a real man, shed real blood to pay for the sins of real, flesh-and-blood people (see Hebrews 9:22), and rose from a real tomb.

This is a truth we must acknowledge to "have the Spirit of God"—to be prepared for Jesus' physical return, when He will rule over His perfectly restored world and people.

Pray:

Thank You, Jesus, for becoming a man. You understand my struggles, though You handled every temptation perfectly. Give me the wisdom and strength to follow Your perfect example.

JESUS IS THE CHRIST

READ LUKE 4:31–41

Key Verse:

Demons also came out of many, crying out and saying, "You are Christ, the Son of God." And He, rebuking them, did not allow them to speak, for they knew that He was Christ.
LUKE 4:41 SKJV

Understand:

- What names did demons apply to Jesus in this passage?
- What does it indicate when evil spirits speak the truth about Jesus?

Apply:

John 7 describes Jewish leaders—angry at Jesus' increasing popularity—sending temple guards to arrest Him during the Festival of Tabernacles. When the guards returned empty handed, the chief priests and Pharisees demanded, "Why have you not brought Him?" (John 7:45 SKJV). The guards simply answered, "No man ever spoke like this man" (verse 46 SKJV).

Jesus possesses the power to create an entire universe (Colossians 1:15–17), so it shouldn't surprise us that the men sent to arrest Him found themselves unable to follow through. In a similar way, even the foul spirits that possessed people in His day would speak truth when confronted with Jesus. Here in Luke 4, demons identify Jesus as "the Holy One of God" and "Son of God" (verses 34, 41 SKJV). In verse 41, demons also called Jesus "Christ," from the Greek *Christos*—equivalent to the Hebrew word *Mashiach* ("Messiah"). Each indicates Jesus' status as God's anointed one, His chosen Savior for the world. This is God's truth, which stands whether someone personally accepts it or not.

As the New Testament writer James noted, even demons believe in God "and tremble" (2:19 SKJV). But that doesn't mean they're saved. We who not only believe in Christ but *trust* in the saving power of His sacrificial death on the cross, however, are born again into God's family.

Acknowledging His truth and making it the core of our being gives us hope in an otherwise hopeless world.

Pray:

Thank You, Jesus, for being the Christ—my hope in this world and for all eternity.

HOW TO RECOGNIZE THE MESSIAH

READ MATTHEW 16:13–18

Key Verses:

"Who do you say I am?" Simon Peter answered, "You are the Messiah, the Son of the living God."
MATTHEW 16:15–16 NIV

Understand:

- Why would Jesus ask the disciples what other people thought about Him?
- Why would Jesus be so complimentary of Peter's answer to the question, "Who do you say that I am?"

Apply:

The twelve disciples' understanding of Jesus unfolded over time. When He called, each one followed—but without a full idea of who this man truly was. Then they saw Him turn water into wine. . .heal people's diseases, both physical and spiritual. . .walk on water. . .feed thousands with a tiny amount of food on two separate occasions.

As part of their training, Jesus asked the disciples, "Who do people say the Son of Man is?"

(Matthew 16:13 NIV). The twelve responded with answers such as the recently executed John the Baptist, back from the dead; Elijah, the famed Old Testament prophet and nemesis of the false god Baal; or one of the more recent prophets of the Jewish exile, like Jeremiah. But when Jesus pressed the disciples by asking, "Who do *you* say I am?" Peter replied with the declaration in today's key verses.

Jesus commended Peter for his understanding but noted an important truth: Peter didn't figure this out himself or learn it from some other wise person; he discerned Jesus' identity only because God had revealed it to him.

Our spiritual discernment, like our salvation, comes from God Himself. As a gift of His grace, our ability to grasp His truth is no reason for pride on our part. If you know that Jesus is the Messiah, God's chosen Savior of humanity, you are blessed like Peter was.

Be grateful.

Pray:

Thank You, Lord, for letting me know You as my Messiah. Please help me to know You more.

HIGH PRIEST FOREVER

READ HEBREWS 7:15–28

Key Verses:

Because Jesus lives forever, his priesthood lasts forever. Therefore he is able, once and forever, to save those who come to God through him.
HEBREWS 7:24–25 NLT

Understand:

- What are the duties of a priest?
- How does Jesus, "the perfect High Priest forever" (Hebrews 7:28 NLT), differ from the Jewish priests of the Old Testament?

Apply:

God gave the family of Aaron—Moses' brother—the duty of being priests to the nation of Israel. They taught God's laws, performed sacrifices for sin, and served as mediators between the Lord and His people. Since they were just as human as the people they represented, the priests had to follow God's rules very carefully. The Old Testament book of Leviticus is an overview of their work.

According to the book of Hebrews, Jesus is a priest not by any descent through Aaron but by "the power of a life that cannot be destroyed"

(7:16 NLT). In that way, Jesus is like Melchizedek, the mysterious "king of Salem and a priest of God Most High" (Genesis 14:18 NLT). Melchizedek blessed Abraham—ancestor of Moses and Aaron and God's people Israel—just like Jesus would bless all of God's people who follow Him by faith.

Like any priest, Jesus explains God's law and encourages people to follow it, serves as a mediator between God and humanity (1 Timothy 2:5), and performed sacrifice for sin.

Notice the past tense of that last verb and the singular nature of the noun *sacrifice*. Unlike the other priests, Jesus Himself was the sacrifice. By His perfect life and substitutionary death on the cross, Jesus was able "once and forever," as today's key verses indicate, "to save those who come to God through him."

This truth changes everything.

Pray:

Thank You for saving me, Jesus. Help me to honor You by my humble obedience.

SALVATION BY NO OTHER NAME

READ ACTS 4:1–20

Key Verse:

"Salvation is found in no one else, for there is no other name under heaven given to mankind by which we must be saved."
ACTS 4:12 NIV

Understand:

- How is Christianity inclusive? How is it exclusive?
- How would you answer the statement "All religions lead to God"?

Apply:

"Inclusion" is modern society's buzzword—though, paradoxically, those shouting loudest for inclusion are often quite exclusionary of viewpoints that differ from their own.

Many people hate Christianity for being "exclusive," and they do have a point. As Peter told a crowd in Jerusalem (a situation described in today's study passage), there is "no other name" besides Jesus by which humans can be saved. And Jesus Himself had taught, "I am the way and the truth and the life. No one comes to the Father except through me" (John 14:6 NIV).

But the Christian faith is also utterly inclusive, in that God would like "everyone to come to repentance" (2 Peter 3:9 NIV). The apostle Paul wrote, quoting the prophet Joel, "Everyone who calls on the name of the Lord will be saved" (Romans 10:13 NIV). Anyone who comes to God through faith in Jesus will be accepted. What's more, Jesus said, "Whoever comes to me I will never drive away" (John 6:37 NIV).

Sadly, not everyone will take advantage of this free salvation. But we who've been called—who have responded in humble belief—are eternally saved and guaranteed every privilege of citizenship in God's kingdom. It all comes down to accepting this truth: Jesus is the only pathway to God, the sole option for human salvation.

Pray:

I believe, Jesus, that You are the way, the truth, and the life—the only access to God the Father. Please help me share this truth with others.

SALVATION: BY GRACE, THROUGH FAITH

READ EPHESIANS 2:1–10

Key Verses:

For it is by grace you have been saved, through faith—and this is not from yourselves, it is the gift of God—not by works, so that no one can boast.
EPHESIANS 2:8–9 NIV

Understand:

- What do many people think will get them into heaven? What does this passage say to them?
- According to this passage, why does God save people?

Apply:

Salvation is simple in concept, yet for many people difficult in practice. That's because our prideful human nature balks at accepting the gift of God's grace—His kindness and favor that we do absolutely nothing to earn. In fact, trying to earn salvation puts us at risk of missing it entirely. It may be simple. . .but only if we do it *God's* way.

No amount of personal sacrifice, no clever

bargaining on our part, no excelling of anyone else's moral qualities can possibly impress God into saving our souls. Otherwise, we would have reason to boast. . .and God despises human pride. All He wants is our faith—our wholehearted belief—in the work of Jesus Christ.

When He reached out to us, we were dead in our sins, unwilling and unable to please Him in any way. We followed our own desires and "were by nature deserving of wrath" (Ephesians 2:3 NIV). But that's where God's mercy and grace came in, lifting us from the pit of sin to the "heavenly realms in Christ Jesus" (verse 6 NIV).

Now, as Christians, we honor God by doing the good works He planned for us eons ago (Ephesians 2:10). But may we never dishonor our Lord by thinking we have in any way earned His love.

Pray:

Lord, I'm grateful for Your grace that led to my salvation. I wasn't deserving of Your love—but now I want to live as worthily as I can.

FAITH IS SHOWN BY WORKS

READ JAMES 2:14–24

Key Verse:

What good is it, my brothers and sisters, if someone claims to have faith but has no deeds? Can such faith save them?
JAMES 2:14 NIV

Understand:

- What do good works by Christians accomplish in this world?
- How do a Christian's good works relate to his salvation?

Apply:

In His omnipotence, God could enact His will in the world purely by His own power. He could miraculously drop hospitals into needy countries, cause food to materialize on the tables of the poor, and engineer lasting peace between warring nations and neighbors. Instead, God typically uses His people's good works to accomplish His plans. As some like to say, we are God's hands and feet.

We have seen that good deeds cannot save a

person. But once that person is saved, good deeds become the order of the day. This is the point the Bible writer James was making, even though the Protestant reformer Martin Luther struggled to accept the letter's legitimacy. Luther felt that words like those in today's key verse contradicted the apostle Paul's teaching that salvation is entirely by faith.

The issue is simply one of timing: Good works do not generate salvation, but true salvation generates good works. To James, a person claiming Christian faith ought to prove it by obeying God's commands—for example, by providing food and clothing for a needy fellow believer. And James also highlighted the example of Abraham, who acted on God's command to sacrifice his son Isaac. Happily for all involved, God stepped in to provide an appropriate animal sacrifice instead (see Genesis 22:1–18).

This is truth to live by: Your good works will never save you. But once you've been saved by faith, you'll express your gratitude by doing whatever God commands.

Pray:

Help me, Lord, to show my saving faith by my selfless service.

SALVATION IS TOTALLY FREE

READ ISAIAH 55:1–9

Key Verse:

*"Is anyone thirsty? Come and drink—
even if you have no money! Come, take your
choice of wine or milk—it's all free!"*
ISAIAH 55:1 NLT

Understand:

- Why do you think some people wrestle with the idea of a totally free salvation?
- Have you ever struggled with that? Why or why not?

Apply:

Today's passage is packed with vital truths. Verse 1 teaches that salvation is purely a gift. Verses 8 and 9 indicate why: God's ways are far beyond our own.

Though we as humans are made in God's image, we reflect only a tiny fraction of who He is. And since Adam and Eve's original sin, that reflection has been marred by our own selfishness and pride.

Even good people have a certain streak of self-interest—a transactional bent that says, "You scratch my back, I'll scratch yours." But God is different. "My thoughts are nothing like your thoughts," He says. "And my ways are far beyond anything you could imagine. For just as the heavens are higher than the earth, so my ways are higher than your ways and my thoughts higher than your thoughts" (Isaiah 55:8–9 NLT).

For reasons we'll never fully understand, the sovereign God allowed a created angel to rebel and gave His created human beings the freedom to follow Satan's disobedience. And then the Lord unveiled a plan of salvation unlike anything the human mind would ever conceive—He Himself would take on human flesh and die a sacrificial death on humanity's behalf. Now, without any cost whatsoever to us other than our humble belief, God offers us salvation. It really is that simple.

That's why disregarding this amazing offer, from this amazing God, carries such heavy consequences. He paid all the cost. . .so we can enjoy all the benefits.

Pray:

Thank You, Lord, for the generosity that makes my salvation available—and totally free. You are so good to me.

TRUTH WE MUST BELIEVE

READ 1 CORINTHIANS 15:1–11

Key Verse:

For I delivered to you first of all what I also received, that Christ died for our sins according to the scriptures.
1 CORINTHIANS 15:3 SKJV

Understand:

- Why is the "good news" (the meaning of the term *gospel*) actually good news?
- What is the importance of the repeated phrase "according to the scriptures" in today's reading?

Apply:

In the epic fantasy *The Lord of the Rings*, Frodo Baggins endures a dangerous journey to toss the far more dangerous Great Ring into the fires of Mount Doom. Early in the quest, he and his loyal companions take a shortcut through the sinister Old Forest, where dark-hearted trees try to lull the hobbits into a deadly sleep. Frodo recognizes trouble, "but the others," author J. R. R. Tolkien wrote, "were too far gone to care."

That's a lot like sin in human lives—it dulls our

senses to the point that we don't even know we're in trouble. But as the apostle Paul wrote in today's key verse, salvation requires us to acknowledge that our moral failures separate us from God. Our sins are why Jesus died on the cross.

God is love (1 John 4:8). It was love that compelled Him to take on human flesh and die for our sin. But to access the full benefit of God's love, we need to approach Him in the way He prescribes—through faith in Christ. And as Paul wrote in Romans 10:17 (SKJV), "Faith comes by hearing, and hearing by the word of God." Hence the repetition of "according to the scriptures" in 1 Corinthians 15:3–4.

To be saved, we must believe the truth that we are sinful creatures. . .and that Jesus came to save us from ourselves. God has made this truth as plain as His presence in creation (see Romans 1:20). So people have no excuse.

Pray:

Lord, I believe—but please increase the depth and passion of my faith.

TRUE SALVATION

READ MATTHEW 7:15–27

Key Verses:

"On judgment day many will say to me, 'Lord! Lord! We prophesied in your name and cast out demons in your name and performed many miracles in your name.' But I will reply, 'I never knew you. Get away from me, you who break God's laws.'"
MATTHEW 7:22–23 NLT

Understand:

- According to Jesus' words in this passage, how can you identify a real Christian?
- By Jesus' standards, how would you assess your own salvation?

Apply:

On a list of scripture's "scariest passages," this one has to rank near the top. According to Jesus Himself, "judgment day" will bring terrible news for certain people. Though they plead with Him to acknowledge the works they did in His name, Jesus will say, "I never knew you. Get away from me, you who break God's laws."

But Jesus wasn't saying we should live in fear,

as if salvation were a roll of the dice. If we're obeying Him, growing His spiritual fruit in our lives (see Galatians 5:22–23), we can be confident that we have built our spiritual houses on a solid rock (Matthew 7:24). No storm or flood can harm a life whose foundation is the Lord Himself.

The key, Jesus taught, is to "actually do" God's will (Matthew 7:21 NLT). And that is achieved by "anyone who listens to [Jesus'] teaching and follows it" (verse 24 NLT).

Unlike the crowds who followed Jesus in person, we today listen to His teaching by reading His unchanging Word. We understand the Father's will by studying what He's laid out for us in scripture. The truth of God's Word provides both the knowledge of salvation and our assurance of it.

Pray:

Thank You, Lord, for the assurance of salvation. Help me to know and obey Your teaching.

REMAIN IN JESUS

READ 1 JOHN 2:18–24

Key Verse:

As for you, see that what you have heard from the beginning remains in you. If it does, you also will remain in the Son and in the Father.
1 JOHN 2:24 NIV

Understand:

- How and why would a person deny that Jesus is the Christ (verse 22), God's chosen Savior of the world?
- When have you seen people desert Jesus? Have you ever been tempted to do so?

Apply:

Many Christians anticipate a satanic world leader, an "Antichrist," who will fulfill the frightening prophecies of Revelation. But today's passage states that "many antichrists" (verse 18) are already here. They're people who deny that Jesus is the Christ, or Messiah.

That describes a strong majority of everyone on earth. But notice that John narrowed his focus to people who "went out from us, but. . .did not really belong to us" (1 John 2:19 NIV). These people were (and are) professing Christians who no longer hold an orthodox—a traditional, biblically supported—view of Jesus.

Sadly, with culture and public morality in free fall, many churched people have chosen to accommodate rather than fight against sin. By doing so, they deny Jesus is the Christ—they portray Him no longer as the Savior from sin but rather as a cheerleader for self-acceptance. Jesus, though, said He did not come to "abolish the Law or the Prophets" (Matthew 5:17 NIV)—the body of teaching that shows what God is like and what He wants in His people. God offers salvation freely, but it's designed to change us into His image, never to leave us in our own.

To be sure of our salvation, we need to remain with Jesus. When you hear "updated" ideas about Him, you can be sure that He isn't the one who's changed.

Pray:

Lord, strengthen me to resist the pressure to change You into an "anything goes" buddy. You are the holy and righteous God!

THE CHRISTIAN LIFE ISN'T EASY

READ 2 CORINTHIANS 4:1–18

Key Verses:

We are troubled on every side, yet not distressed; we are perplexed, but not in despair; persecuted, but not forsaken; cast down, but not destroyed; always bearing about in the body the dying of the Lord Jesus, that the life of Jesus might also be made evident in our body.
2 CORINTHIANS 4:8–10 SKJV

Understand:

- How did you expect your life to change when you accepted Christ?
- How is the Christian life harder than being unsaved? How is it easier?

Apply:

Perhaps it's because we know God is loving and all-powerful that we assume that the Christian life will be easy. As children of the King, we think we'll certainly enjoy a better time in this life.

But experience and scripture both refute that notion. Life in a sinful world is hard, doubly so for

Christians. We face all the typical difficulties plus the animosity of a world that's rebelling against God. Even as great a Christian as the apostle Paul was, he admitted to trouble and perplexity—the daily sensation of dying for Jesus' sake (verse 11). Though these are difficult experiences, Paul—and all of us—can say we are not despairing or destroyed. In fact, our weakness is the opening for Jesus' strength in our lives.

The essential perspective is in verse 16: "We do not lose hope, but though our outward man is perishing, yet the inner man is being renewed day by day" (SKJV). We are moving rapidly toward death, and our enemies attack our bodies, minds, and spirits in every way they can. But in spite of all this trouble, we know that God has a perfect eternity planned for us.

Hardships in this life simply create an inner hunger for our heavenly reward.

Pray:

Heavenly Father, I don't always like trouble in my life, but I know You will use it to make me more like Jesus.

SANCTIFICATION

READ 2 PETER 1:3–11

Key Verse:

Work hard to prove that you really are among those God has called and chosen. Do these things, and you will never fall away.
2 PETER 1:10 NLT

Understand:

- On what things does Peter tell Christians to "work hard" (verses 5–7)?
- How does this hard work relate to your salvation? What does it accomplish?

Apply:

Truth: Salvation is free; sanctification is costly.

Meaning: Jesus did all the work for you to be saved—you simply believe and receive the benefit. But to grow in grace, to be *sanctified*, you'll need to "work hard" as the apostle Peter wrote.

What exactly is sanctification? Old-time Bible commentator Matthew Henry wrote, "It has two things in it, mortification and vivification—dying to sin and living to righteousness, elsewhere expressed by putting off the old man and putting on the new, ceasing to do evil and learning to do well."

We do these things in the power of God's Holy Spirit, informed by God's holy Word. "By his divine power," Peter wrote, "God has given us everything we need for living a godly life" (2 Peter 1:3 NLT). He has provided a Bible full of "great and precious promises," which "enable you to share his divine nature and escape the world's corruption caused by human desires" (verse 4 NLT).

God's Spirit will help at every step of the way, assuring your salvation and empowering your growth, but you are responsible for choosing what's right. That's why Peter uses phrases like "make every effort" and "supplement your faith with. . ." (2 Peter 1:5 NLT). When you do these things—not perfectly but consistently and with a true heart—Peter says you prove that you are really saved. You won't "fall away" from God.

Pray:

Lord, please give me the wisdom and will to deny myself and obey You in everything.

GUIDED INTO GOD'S TRUTH

READ JOHN 16:1–15

Key Verse:

"When he, the Spirit of truth, comes, he will guide you into all the truth. He will not speak on his own; he will speak only what he hears, and he will tell you what is yet to come."
JOHN 16:13 NIV

Understand:

- By what names does Jesus identify the Holy Spirit in this passage? What do those names indicate about the Spirit?
- In what specific ways does the Holy Spirit help followers of Jesus?

Apply:

In John 16, Jesus prepared the twelve disciples for His approaching death, resurrection, and ascension. He warned them of the hatred they would face but assured them that help would come even after He had returned to heaven. This help—the advocate, the Spirit of truth—is His own Spirit, who would arrive on earth in a matter of weeks to live inside believers. Jesus described a coming time (which we as church-age Christians have always known) when God would be intimately and permanently connected to His own.

The Holy Spirit guides believers "into all the truth." This is a deeper knowledge of Jesus, the truth Himself (John 14:6), through a clearer understanding of God's Word, the Bible. Humans can grasp certain truths about God by observing creation (see Romans 1), but our saving and sanctifying knowledge of Jesus comes only through scripture. And scripture is accessible only to the mind that humbly accepts the Spirit's guidance. As the apostle Paul noted, "This is what we speak, not in words taught us by human wisdom but in words taught by the Spirit, explaining spiritual realities with Spirit-taught words. The person without the Spirit does not accept the things that come from the Spirit of God but considers them foolishness, and cannot understand them because they are discerned only through the Spirit" (1 Corinthians 2:13–14 NIV).

Pray:

Holy Spirit, please open my heart to Your guidance.

BELIEVE JESUS, RECEIVE THE SPIRIT

READ ACTS 5:17–32

Key Verse:

"We are His witnesses of these things, and so also is the Holy Spirit, whom God has given to those who obey Him."
ACTS 5:32 SKJV

Understand:

- How does the disciples' behavior in Acts 5 differ from that of a few weeks earlier? (See John 20:19.)
- What accounts for the difference?

Apply:

Shortly before His arrest, trial, and crucifixion, Jesus made a promise to His disciples: Though He would no longer be physically present with them, He would send His own Spirit to live inside them. The Holy Spirit would be their comforter, helper, and advocate (John 14:16, various translations). The Spirit arrived on earth a few weeks later, on the Day of Pentecost, as recorded in Acts 2.

Between those two events, the resurrected-but-not-yet-ascended Jesus told His disciples that the Spirit would enable them to carry the gospel message around the world: "You shall receive power after the Holy Spirit has come on you, and you shall be witnesses to Me both in Jerusalem and in all Judea and in Samaria and to the farthest part of the earth" (Acts 1:8 SKJV). When Jesus returned to heaven, the Spirit took His place on earth—and things changed dramatically for Christ followers. They were (as we are now) indwelt by God Himself, guided and strengthened for the life of faith.

No longer were the disciples in hiding "for fear of the Jews" (John 20:19 SKJV). Now they were boldly telling the leaders who tried to muzzle their witness, "We ought to obey God rather than men" (Acts 5:29 SKJV). This was possible to them because of "the Holy Spirit, whom God has given to those who obey Him."

This is also possible for us.

Pray:

Heavenly Father and Lord Jesus, I thank You for the Holy Spirit You've given me. Help me to walk in His wisdom and power.

GOD IN YOU

READ JOHN 14:15–29

Key Verses:

"I will ask the Father, and he will give you another advocate to help you and be with you forever—the Spirit of truth. The world cannot accept him, because it neither sees him nor knows him. But you know him, for he lives with you and will be in you."
JOHN 14:16–17 NIV

Understand:

- How would you have felt as one of Jesus' twelve disciples, knowing that He would soon no longer be with you?
- How much do you think the disciples understood of what Jesus told them about the Holy Spirit? How well do you understand God's Spirit today?

Apply:

Jesus' disciples couldn't complain that He avoided the issue of His coming death and resurrection. He divulged many details. . .the problem was that the twelve just weren't tracking with Him. At one point, Jesus told the men point-blank, "The Son of

Man is going to be delivered into the hands of men. They will kill him, and after three days he will rise" (Mark 9:31 NIV). Somehow, though, Mark reports that "they did not understand what he meant and were afraid to ask him about it" (verse 32 NIV).

The book of John contains the most detailed accounts of Jesus' words with His chosen followers. His teaching in chapter 14, delivered only hours before His betrayal and arrest, makes it clear that the Holy Spirit—the third person of the Trinity—would actually live inside Christians after Jesus returned to heaven. Though their Lord would no longer be present with them in body, He would absolutely be with them in Spirit—they would not be "orphans" (John 14:18 NIV). This Spirit would not only teach them, reminding them of things Jesus had already shared (verse 26), but grant them peace through His presence (verse 27).

Pray:

Holy Spirit, may I always be a true and pure home for You—God in me.

THE TRUTH ABOUT SINNING

Read Romans 8:5–17

Key Verses:

You have no obligation to do what your sinful nature urges you to do. For if you live by its dictates, you will die. But if through the power of the Spirit you put to death the deeds of your sinful nature, you will live.
Romans 8:12–13 NLT

Understand:

- Why do unsaved people sin? Why do Christians sin?
- What, according to this passage, are several specific benefits of being "controlled by the Spirit" (verse 9)?

Apply:

In the 1960s and 70s, Clerow Wilson, Jr., became one of America's most popular comedians. Better known by his nickname "Flip," Wilson was famous for his catchphrase, "The devil made me do it."

There is some truth in those half-dozen words: Ever since Satan convinced Adam and Eve to disobey God, every one of their descendants has been, by nature, a sinner. As the apostle Paul wrote, "Those who are dominated by the sinful nature think about sinful things" (Romans 8:5 NLT). Unless we humbly accept Christ, we "can never please God" (verse 8 NLT).

But as followers of Jesus—as born-again believers who *have* accepted Christ—we can follow the lead of God's Spirit inside us and say no to the sinful nature that still plagues us. It's a choice *we* must make, though God gives us the inclination and the power. If we fail, it's on us—we can't use the Flip Wilson defense of "the devil made me do it."

But why in the world would we keep sinning? God's Spirit in us gives us true life, helps us kill off our old nature, proves that we are God's adopted sons, and allows us to call Him *Abba*—a term like the English "Daddy."

The truth about sinning is this: You don't have to.

Pray:

Thank You, God, for freedom from sin. Help me to always say yes to Your purity.

TRUE SONS OF GOD

READ GALATIANS 3:23–4:7

Key Verse:

*Because you are his sons, God sent
the Spirit of his Son into our hearts,
the Spirit who calls out, "Abba, Father."*
GALATIANS 4:6 NIV

Understand:

- How were slaves and underage sons similar? How did they differ?
- According to this passage, what happens when a person accepts Christ?

Apply:

In the apostle Paul's day, a well-to-do home might keep a slave to assist with the operations of the household. While the concept is repugnant to modern minds, the Bible acknowledged slavery's reality, urged good treatment of slaves, and described a spiritual freedom in Christ that led to abolition movements in later Western cultures.

Paul, whose treatment of the former slave Onesimus is instructive (see the brief book of Philemon) compared our presalvation status to that of a well-treated slave. We were fed and sheltered and given duties within God's "house"—and in that sense, similar to young sons born into the home.

Though a son "owns the whole estate" (Galatians 4:1 NIV), he is "subject to guardians and trustees until the time set by his father" (verse 2 NIV). We were slaves to God's law, our guardian (3:24), until we came to faith in Christ. But once we are born again (or "come of age," as Paul might say), we gain all the rights of sonship. We're true heirs of the great and powerful God, whom we can now address as "Father."

Even better, we can call God "Abba," the most lovingly familiar term possible. This is due to the generous love of God, who wants "everyone to come to repentance" (2 Peter 3:9 NIV).

If you have received Christ, you are a fully free, completely loved son of God. And if you're still a slave, God offers you adoption into His family today.

Pray:

Lord, I'd much rather be a son than a slave. Thank You for adopting me, Abba Father.

DON'T INTERFERE WITH GOD'S WORK

READ 1 THESSALONIANS 5:12–24

Key Verse:

Do not stifle the Holy Spirit.
1 THESSALONIANS 5:19 NLT

Understand:

- How many commands do you see in this passage?
- What do these exhortations tell you about living the Christian life?

Apply:

In the 1950s and 60s, Campus Crusade for Christ founder Bill Bright developed a witnessing tool called "The Four Spiritual Laws." The first was this: "God loves you and offers a wonderful plan for your life."

That's clearly true, seeing that God the Father sent His own Son to live a perfect human life then die a sacrificial death to pay for your sins. And when you accept this truth by faith, you are saved from those sins, born again, and adopted into God's family. He gives you His Holy Spirit as a guarantee of your current status and your future blessing in eternity.

But you now have a role to play—to learn God's Word and humbly obey it. The Spirit is always present to help you "stay away from every kind of evil" (1 Thessalonians 5:22 NLT), as well as fulfill the other commands in this passage—honor your spiritual leaders, live in peace with other believers, be patient with everyone, do good to all, be joyful and prayerful and thankful.

Your salvation is entirely God's gift to you, delivered by your faith in Christ. But spiritual growth requires your participation, though even this is empowered by God. As you commit to Bible study, prayer, and self-denial, God increases your desire and ability to pursue His righteousness. But if you're lazy, distracted, or rebellious, you interfere with the Holy Spirit's work in your life. You "stifle" Him, or—as Ephesians 4:30 (NLT) says—you "bring sorrow" to Him.

Never interfere with the Spirit's work in your life.

Pray:

Holy Spirit, please guide me into truth and strengthen me to walk in it.

GROWING FRUIT

READ GALATIANS 5:16–26

Key Verses:

But the fruit of the Spirit is love,
joy, peace, long-suffering, gentleness,
goodness, faith, meekness, self-control.
Against such there is no law.
GALATIANS 5:22–23 SKJV

Understand:

- Why would scripture call good Christian behavior "fruit"? What process leads to the development of fruit, literal or figurative?
- Which "works of the flesh" (verses 19–21) occur in your life? Why aren't these called "fruit"?

Apply:

Many people memorize Galatians 5:22–23, right down to the initial "but." That indicates a contrast with what came before—namely, the "works of the flesh" (verse 19).

In stark opposition to the sweet, pleasant "fruit of the Spirit" are attitudes and behaviors like envy, hatred, drunkenness, idolatry, and murder. Few people, thankfully, exhibit all the works listed in verses 19 through 21, but the seed of each is found in every human soul by its native sinfulness. Apart from the Holy Spirit's indwelling, we are naturally characterized by the works of the flesh. They don't grow like spiritual fruit does; the works of the flesh simply *are*.

When we come to Christ for salvation, however, we become "a new creature. Old things have passed away; behold, all things have become new" (2 Corinthians 5:17 SKJV). With our sins wiped away and the Holy Spirit in our lives, we can live differently, peacefully, righteously—though this requires our willing participation.

The apostle Paul wrote, "Walk in the Spirit, and you shall not fulfill the lust of the flesh" (Galatians 5:16 SKJV). Until we are perfected in heaven, we will still feel the deadening pull of our flesh. But by consciously seeking the light of God's Spirit—by watering and fertilizing our soul with scripture and prayer—we will find His fruit growing in our lives.

No fruit springs up overnight, so be patient and persevere. The result is worth it.

Pray:

Spirit of God, please produce an abundance of righteous fruit in me.

YOU ARE GOD'S TEMPLE

READ 1 CORINTHIANS 6:12–20

Key Verses:

Do you not know that your bodies are temples of the Holy Spirit, who is in you, whom you have received from God? You are not your own; you were bought at a price. Therefore honor God with your bodies.

1 CORINTHIANS 6:19–20 NIV

Understand:

- How familiar are you with the saying, "Your body is a temple"? What might that mean?
- What specific sin provides the backdrop for this passage? How does this passage apply to modern life?

Apply:

The Bible clearly teaches that God sends His Holy Spirit to live inside all who truly follow Jesus. In a sense, then, every Christian becomes God's "home" on earth (though we also know from 1 Kings 8:27 that He fills the entire universe). But in 1 Corinthians, the apostle Paul describes believers as a *temple*—not just a house but a place of reverence. While we take care of our own homes, we're likely much more casual in them than at church (an imperfect but useful parallel to the temple). A place devoted to worship deserves special treatment.

That is especially true of our bodies, the temple of God's Holy Spirit. Today's scripture passage deals with sexual sin, a big problem in first-century Corinth just as it is in our world today. "Sexual immorality" (1 Corinthians 6:13 NIV) is not just the physical act with another person but the thoughts and attitudes that lead to such sins. And the apostle Paul's teaching is clear: Don't. "Do you not know that your bodies are members of Christ himself? Shall I then take the members of Christ and unite them with a prostitute?" Paul asked. . .before quickly answering his own question: "Never!" (verse 15 NIV).

(Bonus study: For another "body" that is the Holy Spirit's temple, see 1 Corinthians 3:1–17.)

Pray:

Please keep me pure, Lord, as a worthy temple of Your Spirit.

SELF-DENIAL IS GOOD

READ MATTHEW 16:21–27

Key Verse:

Jesus said to his disciples, "Whoever wants to be my disciple must deny themselves and take up their cross and follow me."
MATTHEW 16:24 NIV

Understand:

- In what areas does our world encourage self-denial? In what areas is self-denial discouraged?
- What did Jesus mean when He said, "Whoever wants to save their life will lose it, but whoever loses their life for me will find it" (verse 25)?

Apply:

Self-denial is not a popular topic nowadays. Occasionally, like John the Baptist crying in the wilderness, someone will call us to limit certain pleasures in the interest of physical, emotional, or spiritual health. But more (and louder) voices shout, "Do what you want! Be yourself! Don't let anyone hold you back!"

For Christians, the key voice is Jesus' own, and

He clearly says, "Tell yourself no."

Why? Because our "fleshly" heart—our flawed, sinful, human core of emotions and desires—is "deceitful above all things" (Jeremiah 17:9 NIV) and will inevitably steer us wrong. It wages continual war against the Holy Spirit inside us. As the apostle Paul wrote, "The flesh desires what is contrary to the Spirit, and the Spirit what is contrary to the flesh. They are in conflict with each other, so that you are not to do whatever you want" (Galatians 5:17 NIV).

As the omniscient God, Jesus understands that our sinful nature craves things that will ultimately destroy us. So He warned people that "saving" one's life in this world (pursuing the pleasures that seem so important in the moment) leads to the loss of eternal life. Conversely, losing our lives now—through self-denial and the crucifixion of our passions—leads to blessing and pleasure forever.

No matter what culture says. . .self-denial is good.

Pray:

Lord, it's not easy to tell myself no. . .but I must. Strengthen me by Your Spirit to follow You completely.

WHOLEHEARTED COMMITMENT

READ LUKE 14:25–33

Key Verse:

"If you want to be my disciple, you must,
by comparison, hate everyone else—
your father and mother, wife and children,
brothers and sisters—yes, even your own life.
Otherwise, you cannot be my disciple."
LUKE 14:26 NLT

Understand:

- How does Jesus describe the "cost" of following Him (verses 26, 33)? What does He mean by that?
- Why would Jesus seemingly discourage people from following Him?

Apply:

Salvation is free and easy for us—Jesus did all the work, which we accept by simple faith. But the Christian life has demands, and the Lord was very up-front about them.

In fact, Jesus was so honest that it almost seems as if He were offering reasons *not* to follow Him.

In this passage, He commanded us to love Him so greatly that our feelings for our closest kin seem like hatred by comparison. Then Jesus offered two examples of "cost counting" that clarify our commitment to Him: Like a man building a tower or a king going to war, do we have the resources to finish successfully? "You cannot become my disciple," He said, "without giving up everything you own" (Luke 14:33 NLT).

Since Jesus is Lord—the unique, almighty, sovereign God of the universe—He demands a wholehearted commitment. He taught another time, "No one can serve two masters" (Matthew 6:24 NLT). As the "jealous God" (Exodus 20:5 NLT), He will not tolerate worshippers with divided loyalties.

Of course, divided loyalties don't allow for true worship anyway. So Jesus basically says, "Come to Me completely. . .or don't come at all."

We are still human, so there will be times when we fail. But our deepest desire must be to know, love, and serve the Lord. If it's not, we should ask ourselves if we truly know Him at all.

Pray:

Lord Jesus, You gave Your life for me—strengthen me to give my all to You.

LEAVING ALL

READ LUKE 5:27–32

Key Verse:

And he left all, rose up, and followed Him.
LUKE 5:28 SKJV

Understand:

- What do you think was included in the "all" that Levi (also known as Matthew) left behind for Jesus?
- How easy or hard is it for you to leave all for Jesus? Why?

Apply:

Had tabloid newspapers existed in first-century Israel, they would have loved Jesus' choice of a tax collector as His disciple. An up-and-coming rabbi selecting a turncoat, a man who demanded money from his fellow Jews for the hated Roman occupiers?

Jesus didn't come to earth to follow convention, though. His mission was to save sinners, a category which includes every human being in history. But only those who acknowledge their sin can enjoy the forgiveness Jesus offers. That's why He said, "I came to call not the [self] righteous, but [admitted] sinners to repentance" (Luke 5:32 SKJV). The tax collector of this passage was willing to own up to his failures.

When Jesus said, "Follow me," Levi left everything to do so. He walked away from his livelihood, one good enough to allow him to make a "great feast" for Jesus "in his own house" (Luke 5:29 SKJV). He left the camaraderie of his tax-collecting fraternity, who undoubtedly banded together against the animosity of their Rome-hating Jewish brothers. But Levi also left behind any guilt he felt over his line of work. . .over any cheating and stealing he'd been part of. . .over any other sin he'd committed, professionally or personally.

Following Jesus means giving up our supposed "right" to anything in our lives. But it also offers the chance to give up the psychological burdens that weigh us down. "Leaving all" may seem frightening, but it's actually freeing.

Pray:

Thank You, Lord, for the two-sided truth of "leaving all" for You. Help me to release everything into Your hands.

TRULY SERIOUS BUSINESS

READ MATTHEW 5:27–30

Key Verse:

"If your right eye causes you to stumble, gouge it out and throw it away. It is better for you to lose one part of your body than for your whole body to be thrown into hell."
MATTHEW 5:29 NIV

Understand:

- How literally should we take Jesus' words in Matthew 5:29? Why?
- What do you think is Jesus' real point in this passage?

Apply:

If someone tells you, "I'm so hungry I could eat a horse," do you throw a Clydesdale on the barbecue? Of course not. His exaggeration is a humorous way of making a point—"I'm really hungry." Food is needed, but a quarter-pound hamburger is sufficient.

Jesus used a similar technique in this section of His famous Sermon on the Mount. He exaggerated to help His hearers (and, today, the readers of His words) to understand the necessity of dealing with adulterous thoughts.

God created marriage as a blessing, both for humanity as a whole and for the countless couples through history who have committed to each other. But things fall apart when spouses look outside their own marriage. Even without physical contact, this is adultery in God's eyes. It's serious business. . .and Jesus says it requires a serious response.

But not self-mutilation. The apostle Paul, who wrote a large portion of the New Testament by the inspiration of Jesus' Holy Spirit, taught that "harsh treatment of the body. . .lack[s] any value in restraining sensual indulgence" (Colossians 2:23 NIV). By His hyperbole, Jesus was saying people—especially us as men—should take extreme measures to avoid adulterous thoughts. Not removing our eyes and hands, but perhaps avoiding certain people, places, and technologies. To paraphrase the Lord's words, "It is better for you to lose a friendship or your cell phone than for your whole body to be thrown into hell."

Pray:

Lord, please help me to take my purity as seriously as You do.

NOTHING COMPARES TO JESUS

READ PHILIPPIANS 3:1–11

Key Verse:

I consider everything a loss because of the surpassing worth of knowing Christ Jesus my Lord, for whose sake I have lost all things. I consider them garbage, that I may gain Christ.
PHILIPPIANS 3:8 NIV

Understand:

- According to this passage, what could the apostle Paul boast about? What did his earthly successes really matter?
- How hard or easy is it for you to "consider everything a loss" compared to knowing Jesus? Why?

Apply:

Some men are so competitive they could turn toothbrushing into an Olympic event. But even the easier going among us can fall prey to the comparison trap, the drive to excel the next guy in order to feel better about ourselves. For Christians, it's all a waste of time.

The apostle Paul played that game—before he met Christ. Then known as Saul, he flaunted his Jewish credentials and passionate pursuit of the Mosaic law. This, he was sure, made him better than other men. . .and more pleasing to God.

But when Saul met Jesus on the road to Damascus (Acts 9), he suddenly realized that his background and achievements mattered not a whit. Human goodness comes only through Jesus Christ, whose perfection becomes ours when we accept it in humble faith. Pride not only interferes with this transaction—it makes it impossible.

As a Christian, Paul would say that everything he'd accomplished in his own strength was like garbage (or "dung," as the King James Version puts it). He had to discard all of those things in order to gain Christ, the ultimate success. Nothing compares to Jesus.

We have the same opportunity and obligation as Paul: Will we consider our own wins as losses to make way for the true victory of knowing Christ?

Pray:

Lord, I give You everything I could ever boast about. Please give me Yourself in return.

IT TAKES HARD WORK

READ 1 CORINTHIANS 9:19–27

Key Verse:

I discipline my body and bring it into subjection, lest that by any means, when I have preached to others, I myself should be disqualified.
1 CORINTHIANS 9:27 SKJV

Understand:

- How often do great achievements come quickly and easily? Why?
- What does the apostle Paul mean when he describes a man "who strives for victory"?

Apply:

These days, you can't avoid advertisements for prescription medicines. And though pills and shots can help to manage certain conditions, a good diet, regular exercise, proper sleep, and a healthy mental outlook are far better for you in the long run. In other words, good health takes hard work.

That is true spiritually as well. There is no miracle drug to immediately make us godly. There is no exciting new pill to keep us there. At salvation, God gives us His Holy Spirit, and then it's on us to put in the hard work. The Spirit is always there to help, but He won't pull us off the metaphorical couch for a workout. We've got to pursue that ourselves.

In today's passage, Paul described his efforts to share the gospel with all types of people. But even such a spiritual giant recognized the dangers of distraction and laziness. So, to achieve the "victory" of seeing people saved and hearing Jesus say "well done" at the end, Paul practiced and encouraged self-control. He said, "I discipline my body"—or, as the New International Version colorfully translates verse 27, "I strike a blow to my body."

This is a difficult assignment. Many times, we'd rather coast along, simply relaxing, consuming entertainment, maybe even pursuing sinful things. But there's no joy in ultimately being disqualified.

It takes hard work to be a successful Christian. Let's get to it.

Pray:

Lord God, give me the wisdom and the will to work hard at Christlikeness.

DEATH TO SELF

READ COLOSSIANS 3:1–14

Key Verse:

So put to death the sinful, earthly things lurking within you. Have nothing to do with sexual immorality, impurity, lust, and evil desires. Don't be greedy, for a greedy person is an idolater, worshiping the things of this world.
COLOSSIANS 3:5 NLT

Understand:

- Besides those listed in verse 5, what other sins must Christians battle?
- Why are these sins still a challenge for believers? How should we address them?

Apply:

In our sin-cursed world, every living thing will die. But until its final moment, life fights for survival. Think of a small animal thrashing and slashing in the jaws of a larger creature, sometimes even inflicting injury on the predator. In a way, that's a picture of our old, sinful nature after we come to Christ.

Though in Christ each of us is a "new person" (2 Corinthians 5:17 NLT), this truth sometimes seems more potential than reality. If we don't fight our old nature, it will destroy us. "Because of these sins," Paul wrote, "the anger of God is coming" (Colossians 3:6 NLT).

That's why God calls us to kill off our old self, to "put to death the sinful, earthly things lurking within." That selfish, warped side of us won't go down without a fight. Our lusts—both for sexual and material things—are powerful even after we're born again. We'll also wrestle with anger, dishonesty, and bad talk (verses 8–9).

But when the Lord calls you to a task, He provides the strength required—and by it you can both kill off your old self and "put on your new nature, and be renewed as you learn to know your Creator and become like him" (Colossians 3:10 NLT). It's doable, but you have to bring a willing heart to God.

Pray:

Please empower me, Lord, to fight my old self. . .to the death.

EXPECT SUFFERING

READ 1 PETER 4:1–7

Key Verse:

Since Christ suffered in his body, arm yourselves also with the same attitude, because whoever suffers in the body is done with sin.

1 PETER 4:1 NIV

Understand:

- Why can suffering be positive? How can ease be a negative?
- Why does Peter call Christians to have a "sober mind" (verse 7)?

Apply:

Perhaps you've read of the newspaper advertisement that supposedly drew hordes of adventurers to Sir Ernest Shackleton's 1914 Antarctic expedition: "Men wanted for hazardous journey. Low wages, bitter cold, long hours of complete darkness. Safe return doubtful. Honour and recognition in event of success."

Researchers haven't located any such notice in periodicals of the time, and many doubt its historicity. But whatever their origin, the words are compelling and lend themselves to our faith journey.

Scripture is very forthcoming about the struggles of being a believer. Jesus promised trouble and persecution in this world (John 15:20; 16:33). Paul, on a daily basis, demonstrated the truth of the Lord's words. Peter too was harassed, arrested, and imprisoned, and tradition says he was ultimately crucified—upside-down, at his request, since he didn't feel worthy of dying like Jesus.

Peter wrote that a willingness to suffer bodily for Christ proves that sin no longer controls us. Once we can cheerfully accept pain on Jesus' behalf, our viewpoint has clearly shifted from this world to the next. Ease and pleasure on earth are temporary. So is suffering, but it leads to an eternity of perfect rest.

Since "the end of all things is near" (1 Peter 4:7 NIV), we are called to be alert and sober. Those qualities enable us to pray—to draw our wisdom and strength from God Himself. No other source can truly carry us through this world's hardships.

Pray:

Lord Jesus, thank You for suffering on my behalf. Strengthen me to suffer for You—and give me confidence in the heavenly reward You promise.

THE TRUTH ABOUT PRAYER

Read Matthew 6:5–15

Key Verse:

"But when you pray, go into your room, close the door and pray to your Father, who is unseen. Then your Father, who sees what is done in secret, will reward you."
Matthew 6:6 NIV

Understand:

- What words in this passage indicate that Jesus simply assumes that prayer will be part of the Christian's life?
- How many prayer instructions do you find in these verses?

Apply:

Christians of all ages, backgrounds, and maturity levels can make the same mistake regarding prayer. As Oswald Chambers, the man behind the classic devotional *My Utmost for His Highest*, explains, "Prayer does not fit us for the greater works; prayer *is* the greater work."

In His Sermon on the Mount, Jesus taught

that prayer is the foundation of our faith life. Three times, He prefaced a teaching with "When [not *if*] you pray" (Matthew 6:5–7 NIV). Then He explained "how you should pray" (verse 9 NIV). What followed is teaching that we now know as "the Lord's Prayer" (verses 9–13).

In a similar passage recorded by Luke, the Lord's Prayer was a response to the disciples' request, "Lord, teach us to pray" (Luke 11:1 NIV). Between the two accounts, we see that, first, every Christian should be praying and, second, praying is a learnable skill.

In fact, Jesus provided several specific instructions, depending on how you choose to count them: Don't draw attention to yourself (Matthew 6:5); pray secretly (verse 6); don't ramble (verse 7); and cover important categories like praise, confession, and requests for physical and spiritual needs (verses 9–13).

All these things add up to our primary work as Christians: connecting with God. What we *do* for Him will flow out of *who we are* within Him.

Pray:

Here I am, Lord. Teach me to pray and help me to make this time a vital part of my day.

PRAYER'S REQUIREMENTS

READ 2 CHRONICLES 7:11–16

Key Verse:

"If My people who are called by My name shall humble themselves and pray and seek My face and turn from their wicked ways, then I will hear from heaven and will forgive their sin and will heal their land."
2 CHRONICLES 7:14 SKJV

Understand:

- How might prayer be compared to a child's interaction with a parent?
- What are the four "if" statements God gives in this passage? What is the "then"?

Apply:

"Why pray," some ask, "if God already knows what I'm going to say?"

It's true that God knows everything, even our own words before we speak them (Psalm 139:4). But in addition to being omniscient (all-knowing), God is a loving Father who enjoys His children's company. Any good dad wants to hear his child's voice, even when he generally knows what he's about to hear.

Two-way love makes the conversation pleasing to both parties.

But no father-child conversation is happy and productive when the son or daughter is selfish or disrespectful. That's why God told Solomon that the Israelites needed to humble themselves, seek the Lord's face, and turn from their evil ways if they wanted His blessing. God presented three scenarios—drought, insect infestation, and disease—that might occur as punishment for the people's sin. But if the people were to humbly and obediently pursue God, He would respond favorably.

Though Jesus has made our interaction with God far different than the ancient Israelites', the requirement for us to show humble respect to our Father certainly still applies. When we pray, let's consciously lower ourselves as we lift up God...and commit to doing whatever He wants us to. Only then will God say, "My eyes shall be open and My ears attentive to the prayer" (2 Chronicles 7:15 SKJV).

Pray:

Lord, You are God—not me. I humbly ask You to empower my obedience.

OBEDIENCE UNLOCKS PRAYER

READ 1 JOHN 3:16–24

Key Verses:

Dear friends, if we don't feel guilty, we can come to God with bold confidence. And we will receive from him whatever we ask because we obey him and do the things that please him.
1 JOHN 3:21–22 NLT

Understand:

- According to this passage, how can we know that God will answer our prayers?
- What does love have to do with answered prayer? How do you define true, biblical love?

Apply:

The human conscience is a powerful, albeit imperfect, guide to better living. God provides people with an inner warning signal that can steer even unbelievers away from moral danger. But the Bible also says the conscience can be seared to the point of death (1 Timothy 4:2). As Christians, we have the Holy Spirit to perfectly guide our conscience, but we must be careful never to override His still, small voice.

When our conscience is clear—when "we don't feel guilty" before God—we can confidently expect His answers to our prayers. And our consciences will be free and blameless when we're living in love toward our fellow Christians.

Just as Jesus gave Himself up for us, so we should for others. It's unlikely that this will ever require our literal death, but John provides an example that hits close to home for most people—giving up money (1 John 3:17). "Dear children," John wrote, "let's not merely say that we love each other; let us show the truth by our actions" (verse 18 NLT). Maybe those actions aren't financial but involve sharing attention, time, or wise guidance. Whatever the need, you as a Christian are called to meet it in ways that align with the unchanging truth of God's written Word. Do these things and expect His answers to your prayers.

Pray:

Heavenly Father, guide me into Your true love for my fellow believers—and let me see powerful answers to my prayers.

GOD'S ANSWERS EXCEL OUR REQUESTS

READ 2 CORINTHIANS 12:1–10

Key Verses:

Three times I pleaded with the Lord to take it away from me. But he said to me, "My grace is sufficient for you, for my power is made perfect in weakness."
2 CORINTHIANS 12:8–9 NIV

Understand:

- When has God answered your prayers exactly as you asked? When has He answered in ways that varied?
- What have you learned from those times when God provided a different answer than you hoped?

Apply:

Imagine a hungry beggar asking a fisherman for part of his catch. Rather than obliging the poor man, the angler hands him a pole and says, "Let me show you how to fish."

That's essentially the old proverb "Give a man a fish and he eats for a day; teach a man to fish and you feed him for a lifetime." It's also an illustration of the way God may respond to our prayers. His answers often excel our requests.

The apostle Paul learned that truth when he asked God to remove the "thorn in [his] flesh" (verse 7 NLT). The Bible never specifies what that problem was—Bible teachers speculate that it may have been poor eyesight, a condition like malaria, a difficult temptation, or even a troublesome person. Whatever the thorn was, God said "no" to its removal but "yes" to something much better: "My grace is sufficient for you, for my power is made perfect in weakness."

In our humanness, we typically think we know what's best for ourselves. But no one knows better than God, and His goals for our lives are far higher than anything we could ever sketch out. Sure, His answers aren't always easy or fun in the moment. But they are undoubtedly the best for us, since they draw us nearer to His heart.

Pray:

Lord, please give me the wisdom to see when Your answers are better than my requests.

NEVER STOP PRAYING

READ DANIEL 6:3–16

Key Verse:

Now when Daniel knew that the writing was signed, he went to his house, and—his windows being open in his chamber toward Jerusalem—he knelt on his knees three times a day and prayed and gave thanks before his God, as he did formerly.

DANIEL 6:10 SKJV

Understand:

- How did jealous rivals choose to attack the godly Daniel? Why were they confident in their approach?
- What can we learn from Daniel's prayer habits?

Apply:

The famous teaching of 1 Thessalonians 5:17 (SKJV)—"Pray without ceasing"—is graphically illustrated in the story of Daniel.

As an elite young Jew at the time of Jerusalem's downfall, Daniel was taken into the court of the Babylonian ruler Nebuchadnezzar. He quickly distinguished himself by courteously requesting a different diet than the royal food and wine. Daniel—along with his Jewish friends now best known by their Babylonian names Shadrach, Meshach, and Abednego—rose into levels of leadership in their new homeland.

Daniel outlived Nebuchadnezzar and his successor Belshazzar, becoming a key figure in the administration of Darius the Mede, who conquered Babylon. Likely now in his seventies, Daniel served so well that rival officials plotted his downfall. But Daniel's integrity forced them to pursue an accusation against him "concerning the law of his God" (Daniel 6:5 SKJV).

They cleverly suggested an "everybody prays only to the king" rule, which Darius foolishly approved. But Daniel kept praying—publicly, three times a day—as he had all along. The king was forced to follow his own law and send Daniel to the lions.

There's a real irony here: Daniel's praying got him both into and out of trouble. God chose to shut the lions' mouths, and Daniel was replaced in the den by his tormentors. . .who were all presumably killed (Daniel 6:24).

No matter what the danger is, never stop praying.

Pray:

Please lead me, Lord, into Daniel's kind of prayer.

PRAYER TAKES FAITH

READ MATTHEW 15:21–28

Key Verse:

"Dear woman," Jesus said to her,
"your faith is great. Your request is granted."
And her daughter was instantly healed.
MATTHEW 15:28 NLT

Understand:

- How would you feel if Jesus responded to you like He initially did to this woman? Why?
- What do you think was Jesus' goal in this interaction?

Apply:

Skeptics are offended by this passage, in which Jesus seems to insult a desperate foreign woman who asks Him for help. Honestly, even some Christians struggle with the story.

The Gentile woman's daughter was possessed by a vicious demon—the likes of which not even Jesus' disciples were able to exorcise (Matthew 15:22–28). But knowing that Jesus could solve her problem, this mom boldly pursued Him—to the point of irritating the twelve.

When Jesus finally acknowledged the woman, He informed her that His mission was to serve God's chosen people, the Jews. She persisted, and Jesus responded with this zinger: "It isn't right to take food from the children and throw it to the dogs" (verse 26 NLT). While many today would gladly trade human beings for dogs, at that time they were considered pests, not pets.

But this mother was dogged—pun intended. And when she answered Jesus' denial with a clever, self-deprecating reply (verse 27), He called her "dear woman" and gave her exactly what she requested. Why? Because, He said, "your faith is great."

We know that Jesus is Savior for all people—this woman just line-jumped ahead of the VIP crowd, most of whom rejected Him anyway. Our Lord's blessing of a non-Jew is great news for the Gentile majority of the world. . .and His answering of her faithful, persistent prayer is a practical takeaway worth our contemplation today.

Pray:

Lord God, help me to pursue You in prayer until I get my answer—or until You direct me to something even better.

PRAYER DEFEATS TEMPTATION

READ MATTHEW 26:31–41

Key Verse:

"Watch and pray so that you will not fall into temptation. The spirit is willing, but the flesh is weak."
MATTHEW 26:41 NIV

Understand:

- What were Peter's failures in this passage? Which other disciples erred in similar ways?
- How surprised was Jesus by the disciples' failure? What was His prescription for their success?

Apply:

The Irish poet and playwright Oscar Wilde (1854–1900) is well known for the quotation "I can resist everything except temptation." The line was spoken by a character in the play *Lady Windermere's Fan*—but it's a sentiment most of us can understand.

So could Peter, one of Jesus' closest friends and the leader of the twelve disciples. On the night

Jesus was arrested, He predicted that His followers would fail: "This very night you will all fall away on account of me," He said (Matthew 26:31 NIV). That's when Peter, famed for impetuosity, insisted that the all-knowing God was wrong. "Even if all fall away on account of you," Peter declared, "I never will" (verse 33 NIV). It was clearly pride that caused Peter to say he would follow Jesus to the death. But "all the other disciples said the same," Matthew reports (verse 35 NIV).

Soon, Jesus had led the twelve to the Garden of Gethsemane, where He would pray for strength to face the ordeal ahead. The Lord took Peter, James, and John, His inner circle, deeper into the garden, asking them to keep watch with Him. Sadly, all three promptly fell asleep.

Truly, they should have followed their Lord's example of prayer, which Jesus soon explicitly stated. "Watch and pray so that you will not fall into temptation," He said. "The spirit is willing, but the flesh is weak."

Pray:

Lord, forgive me for the pride that makes me think I can live for You in my own strength. I'm asking You to help me defeat temptation.

WE NEED GOD'S HELP

READ ROMANS 8:22–32

Key Verse:

Likewise the Spirit also helps our infirmities. For we do not know what we should pray for as we ought, but the Spirit Himself makes intercession for us with groanings that cannot be uttered.
ROMANS 8:26 SKJV

Understand:

- What "infirmities" do we as Christians experience?
- How does God's Holy Spirit address our weaknesses? What is our ultimate hope?

Apply:

Before we came to Christ, we were God's enemies (Romans 5:10). We actively rebelled against Him by disobeying His moral laws.

But even after we're saved, we still struggle with sin. Though we now enjoy "the firstfruits of the Spirit" (Romans 8:23 SKJV) in our lives, our flesh still suffers from many infirmities. Of course, we all experience many temptations every day—to lie, cheat, steal, and lust. We go through moments (or hours, or days) of doubt, fear, and apathy. And in today's scripture, we see that even when we want to do well, "we do not know what we should pray for as we ought."

But God in His goodness provides the help we need—His own Spirit in our lives, interceding for us "according to the will of God" (Romans 8:27 SKJV). With God Himself on our side, who could possibly be against us (verse 31)? It's on us to accept this truth and live up to our high calling. As the apostle Paul wrote, "He who did not spare His own Son but delivered Him up for us all, how shall He not also with Him freely give us all things?" (verse 32 SKJV).

God is pleased to give us the strength to live well in this world. And then He will redeem our bodies (Romans 8:23) for eternal life in a perfect new world.

Pray:

Lord God, I thank You for Your Spirit's prayers on my behalf. Give me the wisdom and will to follow His leading, all the way into eternity.

TRUTH ABOUT THE WORLD

READ 1 JOHN 2:15–25

Key Verse:

Do not love the world or anything in the world. If anyone loves the world, love for the Father is not in them.
1 JOHN 2:15 NIV

Understand:

- What differing loves does John describe in verses 15–17?
- What belief protects Christians and assures them of eternal life?

Apply:

Does 1 John 2:15 contradict John 3:16? Why would John say in today's passage, "Do not love the world or anything in the world" when he also quoted Jesus as saying, "God so loved the world that he gave his one and only Son" (NIV)?

The same Greek word is translated "world" in both verses, but with differing shades of meaning. In John 3, "the world" is the entirety of humanity—needy people to whom a loving God offers salvation through faith in Jesus. In 1 John 2, though, the term refers to the sinful world system, in which people operate by "the lust of the flesh, the lust of the eyes, and the pride of life" (verse 16 NIV). This satanic trio covers every aspect of human selfishness—physical passions, greed, and arrogance. God hates these attitudes and longs to break their power in people's lives.

According to 1 John 2:17 (NIV), this world will pass away, "but whoever does the will of God lives forever." What is the will of God? To accept Christ and be saved. Peter describes God as "not wanting anyone to perish, but everyone to come to repentance" (2 Peter 3:9 NIV). And Jesus declared, "The work of God is this: to believe in the one he has sent" (John 6:29 NIV). That would be Jesus Himself.

"The world" is so bad that Jesus died to purchase our escape. Let's not love any part of this completely messed-up system.

Pray:

Lord, sometimes I'm drawn to things of this world. Please give me a far greater love for You.

THE WORLD HATES TRUE CHRISTIANS

READ JOHN 15:9–25

Key Verse:

"The world would love you as one of its own if you belonged to it, but you are no longer part of the world. I chose you to come out of the world, so it hates you."
JOHN 15:19 NLT

Understand:

- According to Jesus, why are believers hated and persecuted in this world?
- Who loves committed Christians? What benefits are there to true faith in this world?

Apply:

Even as Christians, we're tempted to love this world. Ironically, the world *hates* us.

If we're fully committed to Jesus, we enjoy all the benefits of His love. But neighbors, coworkers, classmates, and even total strangers might very well despise us. Why? Because they have the same satanic attitude that caused people to hate and kill

Jesus Himself. "The world would love you as one of its own if you belonged to it," He said, "but you are no longer part of the world. I chose you to come out of the world, so it hates you." As Jesus' disciple Peter wrote, "You have had enough in the past of the evil things that godless people enjoy—their immorality and lust, their feasting and drunkenness and wild parties, and their terrible worship of idols. Of course, your former friends are surprised when you no longer plunge into the flood of wild and destructive things they do. So they slander you" (1 Peter 4:3–4 NLT).

We shouldn't be surprised by this world's opposition. "Since they persecuted me," Jesus said, "naturally they will persecute you" (John 15:20 NLT). But Jesus also said, "God blesses those who are persecuted for doing right, for the Kingdom of Heaven is theirs" (Matthew 5:10 NLT).

Christ is always with us in this world, and then He will take us to our eternal reward. Stay faithful, because you really can't lose.

Pray:

Keep me by Your side, Lord. I know that's the safest place to be.

BLESSINGS OF PERSECUTION

READ MATTHEW 5:10–16

Key Verse:

"You are the light of the world.
A city that is set on a hill cannot be hidden."
MATTHEW 5:14 SKJV

Understand:

- According to Jesus, what do true believers gain when the world persecutes them?
- How does the faithful Christian's life affect those who seek his harm?

Apply:

With certain exceptions, people don't usually desire hardship and pain. Human nature generally prefers peace, ease, and happiness. Christians, however, are assured of both experiences—trouble in this world, bliss in eternity. We do well to understand this truth.

Jesus guaranteed believers trouble in this life: "In the world you shall have tribulation," He told the twelve (John 16:33 SKJV). Some of that "tribulation"—other translations say "trouble" or "sorrows"—is the natural result of living on a sin-cursed earth that's plagued with disasters, disease, and death. But some of the tribulation is persecution from those who hate Jesus and His message. As He taught in this passage, Christians will be reviled and slandered. . .and worse.

But our troubles only prove Jesus' knowledge of all things. If He could accurately predict such persecution, don't you think His promise of rewards in heaven (Matthew 5:12) is trustworthy too? This makes us "blessed" (verse 10), a word that essentially means "happy."

Oddly enough, the persecution we experience may ultimately benefit our tormentors. If we live up to our Lord's description of believers as "salt of the earth" and "light of the world" (verses 13–14 SKJV), even the hateful, unsaved world will see the difference in our lives and "glorify your Father who is in heaven" (verse 16 SKJV). That may be an enforced worship later on (Philippians 2:10–11). . .but hopefully, the people who see our consistent, obedient example will respond by changing teams now, before it's too late.

Pray:

Help me, Lord, to accept tribulation knowing that You have a perfect eternity planned for me.

DON'T BE LIKE THE WORLD

READ EPHESIANS 5:1–20

Key Verses:

Find out what pleases the Lord.
Have nothing to do with the fruitless deeds
of darkness, but rather expose them.
EPHESIANS 5:10–11 NIV

Understand:

- According to Paul in this passage, how should Christians differ from the world?
- How can true followers of Jesus expose "the fruitless deeds of darkness" (verse 11)?

Apply:

Harry Chapin's 1974 song "Cat's in the Cradle" reached number one on the pop charts and remains a staple of radio rotations today. Called an "anthem of fatherhood" by Aaron Tyler of Onstagemagazine.com, the song describes a young dad whose boy aspires to be just like his father—who, sadly, is too busy with his career to spend much time with his child. By the end of the song, the now-retired dad craves his son's attention, but the young man is consumed with the demands of his own life. The father wistfully realizes that his son has, indeed, become just like him.

Examples—those we follow and those we set—are important. That's why the apostle Paul flatly stated, "Follow God's example" (Ephesians 5:1 NIV). We'll be set apart from the sinful world since we won't be sexually immoral or greedy or obscene, among other things (verses 3–4). By following God and avoiding poor attitudes and behaviors, we can "live as children of light" (verse 8 NIV). This sets a good example for everyone around us.

Part of our example should be exposing the "fruitless deeds of darkness." We do this not through high-handed moralizing but by humbly and compassionately showing people a better way. The unsaved world will often resent us as Christians. . .but that should be for our good character, not for the harshness of our judging.

Consistent Christian living may cause sinful people to want to become just like us.

Pray:

May I follow Your example, Lord, and set a consistently good and attractive example for the unsaved world.

THIS WORLD IS DANGEROUS

READ ACTS 2:29–41

Key Verse:

With many other words he warned them; and he pleaded with them, "Save yourselves from this corrupt generation."
ACTS 2:40 NIV

Understand:

- What two key figures did Peter emphasize in this passage? How do they relate and compare to each other?
- How is our generation "corrupt"? How can we save ourselves from it?

Apply:

The second chapter of Acts is well known for recording the Holy Spirit's arrival on the day of Pentecost. After the resurrected Jesus returned to heaven, He fulfilled the promise He'd made to send back the Spirit to live inside Christians, empowering them to reject sin and faithfully follow Jesus.

The result of this outpouring was one of the

Bible's most powerful sermons, preached by the apostle Peter. Having fearfully denied Christ only a few weeks before, the newly Spirit-filled Peter urged the residents of Jerusalem to believe and receive Jesus. These people were part of a culture that had crucified the Lord and Messiah (Acts 2:36). That's why Peter cried, "Save yourselves from this corrupt generation."

Jesus came from the family line of the beloved King David, yet He far exceeded David. Only He could save the people from their sins, if and when they would repent of (turn from) them.

Our own generation is just as corrupt and dangerous as Peter's. Considering the greed and oppression and bloodthirstiness of our culture, it's not hard to imagine our own fellow man crucifying Jesus. And apart from His Holy Spirit, we might very well be in the shouting mob ourselves.

This world is dangerous. The only way to "save yourself" is to humbly permit Jesus to do that. Then, allowing His Holy Spirit to control your thoughts and actions, you cannot only survive this world but rise above it.

Pray:

Lord Jesus, I humbly acknowledge Your lordship in my life. Please save me from this corrupt generation.

WORLD'S FRIEND, GOD'S ENEMY

READ JAMES 4:1–10

Key Verse:

Don't you realize that friendship
with the world makes you an
enemy of God? I say it again: If you
want to be a friend of the world,
you make yourself an enemy of God.
JAMES 4:4 NLT

Understand:

- According to this passage, what does "friendship with the world" look like?
- What is James' prescription for rejecting friendship with the world?

Apply:

Many Bible scholars believe James is the New Testament's oldest book, written only twelve years after the death and resurrection of Christ. The author is thought to be Jesus' half brother James (Matthew 13:55; Mark 6:3), who didn't initially believe (Mark 3:21; John 7:5) but ultimately became a leader of the early church at Jerusalem (Galatians

2:1–10). Since the letter was written to Jewish believers steeped in the law, James emphasized how saving faith plays out in behavior—especially in visible things like good deeds.

On the other hand, negative attitudes and behaviors like jealousies and quarrels (James 4:1–2) are visible things that call our faith into question. If we squabble with others and seek our own selfish pleasures, it shows that we love the world more than we love God. James was crystal clear on that: "If you want to be a friend of the world, you make yourself an enemy of God."

Though our salvation comes entirely from the Lord, our *sanctification*—growth in grace—demands our participation. So James lays out several practical choices we must make to confirm we're on God's side rather than the world's: Humble yourself (James 4:7). Resist the devil's advances (verse 7). Purify your heart (verse 8). Take sin seriously, to the point of shedding tears (verse 9).

When you do these things, God "will lift you up in honor" (verse 10 NLT).

Pray:

Help me to humble myself before You, Lord—I don't want this world to control my thoughts and actions.

ESCAPING THE WORLD'S CORRUPTION

READ 2 PETER 1:2–11

Key Verses:

His divine power has given to us all things that pertain to life and godliness, through the knowledge of Him who has called us to glory and virtue, by which are given to us exceedingly great and precious promises, that by these you might be partakers of the divine nature, having escaped the corruption that is in the world through lust.

2 PETER 1:3–4 SKJV

Understand:

- According to Peter, what is the reward for escaping the world's corruption?
- What specific commands does Peter give to fight off the world's corruption?

Apply:

Peter wrote nearly two thousand years ago, but he described our modern world perfectly. Terms like *corruption* and *lust*, when applied to our society, seem more and more accurate each day.

God isn't surprised by our world's condition,

and He chose to put each one of us right where (and when) we are. Like the Old Testament queen Esther, you're alive "for such a time as this" (Esther 4:14 SKJV).

Right now, you can partake of the divine nature by consciously adding good things to the foundation of your faith in Christ: virtue (choosing to do right), knowledge (studying God's Word), self-control (saying no to your own desires), patience (accepting God's ways and timing), godliness (acting as Jesus did), brotherly kindness (caring for other people), and love (selflessly giving up your time, energy, and resources).

"If these things are in you and abound," Peter wrote, "they make you that you shall be neither barren nor unfruitful in the knowledge of our Lord Jesus Christ" (2 Peter 1:8 SKJV). And they unleash His "exceedingly great and precious promises" in your life.

Pray:

Help me, Lord, to do my part, since You have done Yours. I'm saved by Your grace; may my conscious choices and hard work add the virtues that help me escape this world's corruption.

DEFEATING THE WORLD

READ 1 JOHN 5:1–12

Key Verse:

Who can win this battle against
the world? Only those who believe
that Jesus is the Son of God.
1 JOHN 5:5 NLT

Understand:

- What does our obedience to God's commands prove? What does it accomplish?
- What is the basis of our obedience to God?

Apply:

Our world's evil can be overwhelming. We see corruption in every realm of society—political, business, educational, you name it—and we think, *What can I do? I'm only one person.* Then we recognize the corruption in our own hearts and begin to despair.

But Christians always have hope. John states very clearly that belief in Jesus as the Son of God allows us to "win this battle against the world." When we acknowledge Jesus as the Christ—as God's chosen and anointed Savior of the world—we become God's children (1 John 5:1). He gives us a new birth, sealing us by His Holy Spirit in our lives, and we find that obedience to His rules is "not burdensome" (verse 3 NLT). We become able to love God and other people, and we find victory over all the dark elements of the world and of our own hearts. "Every child of God defeats this evil world," John wrote, "and we achieve this victory through our faith" (verse 4 NLT).

As in any war, there will be battles lost—and that's why 1 John provides guidance on confessing our sins and being restored to fellowship with God (1:8–9). But our ultimate victory is assured by God Himself because of the faith we've put in the second person of the Trinity—His perfect Son, Jesus Christ. Through Him, we have an eternal, indestructible life (1 John 5:11). . .no matter what the world throws our way.

Pray:

Thank You for this promise of victory, Lord. Help me to cling to this promise and live in obedience.

FIGHT FOR THE FAITH

READ JUDE 3–10

Key Verse:

Although I was very eager to write to you about the salvation we share, I felt compelled to write and urge you to contend for the faith that was once for all entrusted to God's holy people.
JUDE 3 NIV

Understand:

- How would you define "the faith"? What does it mean to "contend" for it?
- How can Christians both love their enemies and fight for faith?

Apply:

Perhaps you've heard Christians say, "God doesn't need us to defend Him." In one sense, that's true—God, being God, doesn't need a single thing outside of Himself. He is perfectly whole, good, and capable apart from any human input.

And yet in His Word, He's called Christians to "contend for the faith"—the biblical record and gospel message that reflect who and what He is. Scripture is His self-revelation, a humanly understandable account of the infinite God's workings.

Without the Bible, we would lack the knowledge we need to be saved from sin. We couldn't understand God's desire for our devotion—which is what gives purpose to our lives.

As God's sworn enemy, Satan wants nothing more than to destroy that faith. . .or at least just warp the message enough to keep people from truly following Jesus. If he can, the devil wins souls for hell. Misery does love company.

So God gives us the job of contending for the faith. We must study and know it ourselves, share it consistently, and correct false teaching when it arises. By doing so, as Paul wrote to Timothy, "you will save both yourself and your hearers" (1 Timothy 4:16 NIV).

Pray:

I pray, Lord, paraphrasing verses 20–21 of Jude, that I may build myself up in my most holy faith, keeping myself in Your love as I wait for the mercy of my Lord Jesus Christ to bring me to eternal life.

STAND FAST—TOGETHER

READ PHILIPPIANS 1:21–30

Key Verses:

Only let your conduct be as is proper for the gospel of Christ, that whether I come and see you or else be absent, I may hear of your affairs, that you stand fast in one spirit, with one mind striving together for the faith of the gospel, and in nothing terrified by your adversaries, which is to them an evident sign of destruction, but to you of salvation, and that from God.
PHILIPPIANS 1:27–28 SKJV

Understand:

- What was Paul's desire for himself in this passage? For the Philippian believers?
- What does Christian unity entail? What does it accomplish?

Apply:

Philippians, a letter emphasizing joy, was written from a Roman prison. Paul, who experienced severe hardships while serving Jesus, had credibility when he urged his readers to suffer well for Christ (Philippians 1:29).

Paul candidly admitted that he was ready to

"depart and to be with Christ" (Philippians 1:23 SKJV). But he also knew that this decision was in God's hands—and was happy to live on for the Philippians' sake. As you read in today's key verses, he longed for those believers (and by extension, all of us) to stand fast in the faith, fearlessly striving together for the gospel.

The key word here is *together*.

While many aspects of the Christian faith are personal, some are communal—God knew we would need support to live successfully in an antagonistic world. By maintaining unity in the essentials of our faith—the black-and-white truths of God's written Word—we find the strength to stand tall like Shadrach, Meshach, and Abednego as everyone around us bows. Our Spirit-led confidence will show the unsaved their error. . .and will hopefully lead them to Christ.

Pray:

Lord, I'd like to be as confident and courageous as Paul. May I find support in my Christian community and offer it back in return.

TRUE VERSUS FALSE MOTIVES

Read Philippians 1:12–18

Key Verses:

It is true that some preach Christ out of envy and rivalry, but others out of goodwill. . . . But what does it matter? The important thing is that in every way, whether from false motives or true, Christ is preached.

Philippians 1:15, 18 niv

Understand:

- What good came out of Paul's persecution and imprisonment?
- How could Paul conduct himself without jealousy? How can you?

Apply:

Have you ever noticed how often the New Testament mentions false teachers, false prophets, false apostles, and false believers? True Christians must always be on guard against Satan's counterfeits. It stands to reason that the "father of lies" (John 8:44 niv) would try to wreck Jesus' church with confusion arising from fellow "Christians."

The apostle Paul felt the trouble these false Christians caused. While he was imprisoned for his faithful gospel preaching, they were preaching out of "envy and rivalry" (Philippians 1:15 NIV) and creating problems for Paul (verse 17). But despite being surrounded by swirling jealousy, Paul could sense a Romans 8:28 result. God was making all things work together for good, using the trouble-makers' message to further the truth of Jesus Christ.

What's more, all this attention on Paul caused many people—even his prison guards—to realize he was suffering for Jesus' sake. This gave many other true believers confidence to speak boldly of their own faith (Philippians 1:13–14). And in that, Paul could rejoice.

Today, we see many people claiming the name of Christ but not living by His Word—even causing trouble for those of us who do. Let's make Paul our example, faithfully representing Jesus whatever our circumstances and thanking Him for the good He's doing in, through, and around us.

Pray:

Lord, I dislike the world's dishonesty, especially when it infiltrates Your church. Help me to always be faithful, no matter how false anyone else is.

SPEAK UP FOR GOD'S TRUTH

READ TITUS 1:10–16

Key Verses:

So reprimand them sternly to make them strong in the faith. They must stop listening to Jewish myths and the commands of people who have turned away from the truth.
TITUS 1:13–14 NLT

Understand:

- Do you think much of contemporary preaching has the same sternness as Paul's words in this passage? Why or why not?
- What is the relationship between words and actions in the Christian life (verse 16)?

Apply:

The Bible calls Christians to be many things: honest, pure, compassionate, generous, faithful, wise. One thing God never demands of believers is that they be nice—that is, if *nice* follows the contemporary definition of quiet, passive, and affirming of false teaching and sin.

The apostle Paul urged his young associate

Titus to "reprimand" his congregation "sternly" to head off the false teaching that had gained a foothold in the church in Crete. Some professing Christians were defaulting to their former Jewish beliefs and arguing that Christians needed to be circumcised. Paul, adamant that nothing should ever be added to faith in Christ, urged Titus to boldly condemn this false teaching.

Paul immediately knew what many of us are only now coming to realize: A little compromise, left unaddressed, soon leads to major problems in the beliefs and behaviors of individuals, churches, and Christian organizations. As he wrote another time, "False teaching is like a little yeast that spreads through the whole batch of dough!" (Galatians 5:9 NLT).

Standing for God's truth demands that we weigh the words and actions of everyone—including ourselves. And if there's any disconnect, we must speak up for what's right. We dare not allow creeping falsehoods to make us "worthless for doing anything good" (Titus 1:16 NLT).

Pray:

Lord, please give me the wisdom to know Your truth and the boldness to speak up for it.

CONFRONTATION

Read Galatians 2:11–14

Key Verse:

But when I saw that they did not walk uprightly according to the truth of the gospel, I said to Peter before them all, "If you, being a Jew, live according to the manner of Gentiles and not as the Jews do, why do you compel the Gentiles to live as the Jews do?"
Galatians 2:14 SKJV

Understand:

- Have you ever confronted (or been confronted by) a fellow believer over some bad behavior? How did that go?
- Why might even the great apostle Paul have decided against addressing this situation? Why did he choose to plow ahead?

Apply:

Some people thrive on confrontation. But it's safe to assume most would prefer to avoid it. Even when another person's choices are causing discomfort, many of us take the route of "peace," staying silent and hoping the situation resolves itself.

But on moral and theological issues, God

doesn't give us that luxury. In today's passage, the apostle Paul called a foul on his own team, opposing Peter "to the face because he was to be blamed" (Galatians 2:11 SKJV).

At issue was the historical Judaism of the new Christian church. God had given Peter a vision assuring him of the Gentiles' place in the body of Christ (Acts 11:1–18). Peter took that to heart and fellowshipped with Gentile Christians in Antioch. . .until some circumcised Jewish Christians came to town. Then he buckled to the Jews' traditional shunning of Gentiles. When the acknowledged leader of Jesus' apostles went soft, other Jewish Christians—even Barnabas, the "Son of Consolation" (Acts 4:36 SKJV)—backed away too.

But Paul, sensing the damage this could do to the fledgling church, immediately spoke up. He confronted the issue and Peter himself, the latter's long history with Jesus notwithstanding. It's probably no exaggeration to say that Paul saved the church from irreparable harm.

Pray:

Lord, give me courage to speak up whenever You prompt me to.

YOUR TRUE DEFENSE

READ MATTHEW 10:16–20

Key Verses:

"But when they arrest you, do not worry about what to say or how to say it. At that time you will be given what to say, for it will not be you speaking, but the Spirit of your Father speaking through you."
MATTHEW 10:19–20 NIV

Understand:

- How often do you think about the possibility of serious persecution? How confident are you in your ability to defend the faith?
- According to Jesus in this passage, how does any believer speak clearly in stressful situations?

Apply:

"Acts" is short for "The Acts of the Apostles," and the book does describe the experience of men like John, Peter, and Paul. But it also includes a substantial account about Stephen—not an apostle but rather one of the first deacons. He was known as "a man full of faith and of the Holy Spirit" (Acts 6:5

NIV) and became the church's first martyr.

By God's power, Stephen performed miracles as he served. Before long, jealous Jews arrested him on false charges of blasphemy. Hauled in front of the Jewish high court, Stephen was serene—"his face was like the face of an angel" (Acts 6:15 NIV).

That was evidence of the Holy Spirit in Stephen's life, as was his powerful speech defending God's truth. Throughout fifty-two verses, Stephen explained how Jewish history pointed toward Jesus Christ. Then he accused his captors of disobeying God's law by betraying and murdering their Messiah.

Stephen's speech fulfilled Jesus' words in today's key verses, and the enraged mob killed him in response (Acts 7:59–60). The intense persecution that followed scattered the believers, who then took the gospel to new locations—and launched the church on a worldwide trajectory.

Pray:

Heavenly Father, I don't want to be persecuted—but if and when it comes, please give me Your words.

YOU CAN'T FIGHT ALONE

READ EPHESIANS 6:10–18

Key Verse:

Put on salvation as your helmet, and take the sword of the Spirit, which is the word of God.
EPHESIANS 6:17 NLT

Understand:

- How many ways do these verses indicate that you need God's help to battle the world?
- Have you ever been tempted to "go it alone" in the spiritual realm? Why or why not?

Apply:

"Never in the field of human conflict," British Prime Minister Winston Churchill declared in August 1940, "was so much owed by so many to so few." He was honoring the Royal Air Force, which was then opposing the Nazi air assault in the Battle of Britain. The defenders' courage and skill helped stave off a planned German invasion of the island nation.

But England's victory wasn't entirely her own—according to the Royal Air Force Museum, one-fifth of the crew members came from overseas. Airmen represented sixteen countries: Commonwealth citizens from Canada, Australia, New Zealand, and South Africa participated by the dozens, as did a handful from places like Rhodesia, Jamaica, and Barbados. Europeans from Poland, Czechoslovakia, France, and Belgium volunteered, along with numerous Americans, who formed three "Eagle Squadrons" within the RAF.

In our spiritual battles, we as Christians need assistance as well—and in far greater proportions than 20 percent. Our entire strength is in the Lord (Ephesians 6:10), and our protection is the armor He provides (verses 11–17). Before and during every battle, we must pray in God's Spirit (verse 18). Only then can we "resist the enemy in the time of evil" (verse 13 NLT).

May we never foolishly (and pridefully) think we're strong enough on our own. As Paul warned elsewhere, "If you think you are standing strong, be careful not to fall" (1 Corinthians 10:12 NLT).

Pray:

Heavenly Father, I need Your mighty power. May I humbly don Your armor and fight in Your strength.

TIMOTHY'S CHARGE (AND YOURS)

Read 1 Timothy 6:11–21

Key Verses:

Timothy, guard what has been entrusted to your care. Turn away from godless chatter and the opposing ideas of what is falsely called knowledge, which some have professed and in so doing have departed from the faith.
1 Timothy 6:20–21 NIV

Understand:

- What exhortations does Paul have for Timothy? What "command verbs" are used in this passage?
- Where do God's empowerment and our obedience intersect?

Apply:

This passage provides a thumbnail sketch of the entire Christian life—a summary of God's truth, on and for which we stand.

The apostle Paul urged his young associate to "flee" (1 Timothy 6:11 NIV) the love of money he'd warned about in verses 7–10. Paul commanded him to "pursue" virtuous traits, "fight" the good fight of faith, and "take hold" of his eternal life (verses 11–12). He expected Timothy "to keep this command without spot or blame until the appearing of our Lord Jesus Christ" (verse 14 NIV).

Timothy was commanded to teach truths he was certainly expected to obey himself: to put his hope in God rather than in money (verse 17) and to do good (verse 18). Then, as seen in today's key verses, Timothy was urged to "guard what has been entrusted to your care"—the gospel message handed down from Jesus to the apostles to successive generations of believers. Silly arguments and esoteric philosophies that confuse God's simple truth should be shunned.

Scripture teaches that God draws people to Himself, giving them even the faith to accept His gift of salvation (Ephesians 2:8). But though these blessings of grace are free, once saved we must work to "grow in the grace and knowledge of our Lord and Savior Jesus Christ" (2 Peter 3:18 NIV).

Timothy's charge is also our own.

Pray:

Thank You, Lord, for saving me. Now empower me to stay the course, obeying Your Word without spot or blame.

YOU WILL BE REWARDED

READ GENESIS 15:1–6

Key Verse:

After these things the word of the
LORD came to Abram in a vision, saying,
"Do not fear, Abram. I am your shield
and your exceedingly great reward."
GENESIS 15:1 SKJV

Understand:

- How "sensible" was God's promise of many descendants to Abram? Why?
- How did Abram respond to God's promise? What did Abram get in response?

Apply:

Genesis 15 is a familiar passage containing the Bible's classic explanation of faith: The man who would later be called Abraham "believed in the LORD, and He counted it to him for righteousness" (verse 6 SKJV).

God had chosen Abram from a people who worshipped false gods (Joshua 24:2–3), promising to make him the patriarch of a large family—a great nation—that would bless the entire world. It was almost incomprehensible, seeing that Abram was seventy-five years old and childless (Genesis 12:1–4).

But he obeyed God's command to leave his idolatrous homeland and go "to a land that I will show you" (Genesis 12:1 SKJV). By the time God reiterated His promise in Genesis 15, Abram had sojourned in Egypt to escape a famine, returned to the land God had promised, built up great wealth in goods and flocks, and rescued his nephew Lot, who had been captured in a war between local kings. Yes, Abram was still childless and even older now. But having already experienced several proofs of God's faithfulness, he still believed what he could not see (Hebrews 11:1). And that made him righteous in God's eyes.

In time, Abram would get the child—and the numerous descendants—that God had promised. But don't overlook the everlasting blessing that he also received immediately: God Himself as a protective "shield," plus a relationship with God as Abram's "exceedingly great reward."

Pray:

Lord God, please remind me that my ultimate reward isn't heaven in the future—it's You, now and forever.

REWARDS, NOW AND LATER

READ MARK 10:17–31

Key Verses:

"Everyone who has given up house or brothers or sisters or mother or father or children or property, for my sake and for the Good News, will receive now in return a hundred times as many houses, brothers, sisters, mothers, children, and property—along with persecution. And in the world to come that person will have eternal life."
MARK 10:29–30 NLT

Understand:

- What is the context of Jesus' words in Mark 10:29–30? Why was He discussing money and possessions?
- What do we receive in return for surrendering our lives to Jesus?

Apply:

The Bible consistently urges compassion for the poor. But it never forbids wealth, either. Abraham, Job, and Solomon are remembered for their riches, though it must be noted that possessions could not keep them from all trouble. Solomon himself said, "Riches won't help on the day of judgment, but right living can save you from death" (Proverbs 11:4 NLT).

The man who approached Jesus in today's passage struggled to accept Solomon's words. Often called "the rich young ruler"—a name patched together from parallel accounts in Matthew, Mark, and Luke—this man walked away from life with Jesus rather than giving up the wealth that possessed him.

Jesus promises eternal life in a place where gold is used as paving material (Revelation 21:21). But He also offers plenty of good things in this world too—though in ways that might surprise us.

When we give up family, friends, and possessions for Him, Jesus returns "a hundred times as many." How? By the love and generosity of His worldwide family, who become our "brothers or sisters or mother or father or children" and make available their homes and food and other belongings. It appears that accessibility trumps ownership—but we are rewarded generously either way. And then eternal life follows.

Pray:

Thank You for being so generous, Lord. May I never stress over mere things.

YOU WILL BE AVENGED

Read Psalm 58:1–11

Key Verse:

Then people will say, "Surely the righteous still are rewarded; surely there is a God who judges the earth."
Psalm 58:11 NIV

Understand:

- When have you wished for vengeance on an enemy? Why?
- How is God's vengeance on the wicked a reward to the righteous?

Apply:

Vengeance is a powerful—and common—human desire. Why else would so many movies and television shows emphasize the bad guys "getting their due"?

We've all, at some point, experienced mistreatment that created a longing for vengeance. But it doesn't take a Bible scholar to know that we as Christians are called to love our enemies (Matthew 5:44) and pray for their well-being, no matter how much hatred or persecution they throw our way. God is unhappy when human beings gloat over another's misfortune (Obadiah 12–13), so we need to tread very carefully through this minefield.

However. . .it's certain that God Himself, through His perfect knowledge and in His perfect justice, will avenge His faithful people.

Psalm 58 conveys the complaint and the confidence of David, who suffered much persecution—even from the God-ordained King Saul, who did not always "speak justly" or "judge people with equity" (verse 1 NIV). But David realized that God would ultimately repay evil (verse 11). That's why, when presented with opportunities to end the king's persecution once and for all, David could spare Saul's life. . .twice (1 Samuel 24, 26).

God's desire is that all people come to repentance (2 Peter 3:9). So, some enemies may ultimately become brothers, with the punishment they deserve falling on Jesus Christ. But know that God will deal with the others according to their sin, while your faithfulness to Him will be perfectly and amply rewarded.

Pray:

Lord, I look forward to Your perfect justice. But for now, I ask You to convict my enemies and turn them into friends.

RESURRECTION IS REAL

READ ACTS 17:22–33

Key Verse:

When they heard Paul speak about the resurrection of the dead, some laughed in contempt, but others said, "We want to hear more about this later."
ACTS 17:32 NLT

Understand:

- According to the apostle Paul in this passage, why is Jesus' resurrection so important?
- What does the fact of Jesus' resurrection mean to people in general?

Apply:

Athens of the apostle Paul's day confirms the observation that many people have made over the centuries: Human beings are compelled to worship. The question is always what or who the object of that worship will be.

Christians have come to understand—by God's grace—that only He is worthy of worship. Apart from this grace, however, broken humanity will worship anything else: idols, health, money, sex, celebrities, you name it. In polytheistic Athens, the residents even acknowledged an "unknown god."

Paul was happy to introduce these people to the one true God, who came to earth to live and die as a man named Jesus. And all the things God had said—about creation and the Creator, about human sin and divine salvation, about coming judgments and rewards—was powerfully confirmed by the resurrection of Jesus Christ. Only the one true God could swing something so audacious and amazing.

Many of the Athenians, caught up in their education and "wisdom," scoffed at the idea. But others were intrigued enough by the concept to say, "We want to hear more about this."

If you have chosen to follow Christ, you have gone a step farther than even those open-minded Athenians—you have committed yourself to the God who proved His absolute power over the strongest, most fearsome aspect of this world: death. And you have welcomed that power into your own life, both now and forever.

Pray:

Lord, I believe in Your power, a power that exceeds even death. Please employ that power in my life today.

THE TRUTH OF OUR OWN RESURRECTION

Read 1 Corinthians 15:35–49

Key Verse:

As we have borne the image of the earthly, we shall also bear the image of the heavenly.
1 Corinthians 15:49 skjv

Understand:

- What does the apostle Paul say about the resurrection of those who believe in Jesus?
- What other Bible passages may help to "fill in the blanks" of Christians' resurrection?

Apply:

With only three biblical exceptions—Enoch, Elijah, and those living believers who will someday be "caught up. . .in the clouds to meet the Lord in the air" (1 Thessalonians 4:17 skjv)—every human being dies. And every human being is destined for resurrection, "both the just and the unjust" (Acts 24:15 skjv). The latter, in Jesus' words, "shall go away into everlasting punishment, but the righteous into eternal life" (Matthew 25:46 skjv).

Jesus' own resurrection proves His power to give life to His followers. Though death is our destiny on earth, life is the legacy for Christians. But we may wonder, as Paul's contemporaries did, what exactly that looks like.

Using a readily understandable example, Paul said our physical bodies would be "sown" like seed, buried lifeless in the ground. But God's power will cause us to grow, like a stalk of grain from a single germ of wheat, into something far greater and more productive. Our resurrection bodies won't be exactly like our earthly bodies—they'll be much better.

Jesus' resurrected body provides intriguing clues to our own. He was physical, able to eat (Luke 24:42–43) and be touched (John 20:27). He was recognizable as Himself, at least when He chose to be (Luke 24:13–35; John 20:15–16). But He could also move through locked doors (John 20:19) and ascend through the sky into heaven (Acts 1:9–11).

Clearly, amazing things await us.

Pray:

Lord, I look forward to a glorified body that never breaks down or dies—but can serve You forever.

ETERNITY

Read Revelation 21:22–22:7

Key Verses:

No longer will there be any curse. The throne of God and of the Lamb will be in the city, and his servants will serve him. They will see his face, and his name will be on their foreheads.

Revelation 22:3–4 NIV

Understand:

- What "curse" will be absent from the Christian believer's eternity?
- According to this passage, what will followers of Jesus do in eternity?

Apply:

God has planned "a new heaven and a new earth" (Revelation 21:1 NIV) for those who follow Jesus—the people "whose names are written in the Lamb's book of life" (verse 27 NIV).

In this perfect place, the curse that resulted from Adam and Eve's sin will be banished. No longer will there be thorns and thistles, painful labor, and death (Genesis 3:17–19). Instead, trees will produce fruit year-round, life-giving water will flow unimpeded, and God Himself will provide unending light.

Unlike the jokes and cartoons that depict people in heaven sitting on clouds and strumming harps for eternity, we will have jobs to do. We will "serve" God the Father and Jesus Christ, His "Lamb." And, along with God, we will "reign for ever and ever" (Revelation 22:5 NIV). Exactly what that entails remains to be seen, but we can be sure it's good—especially since the book of Revelation specifies that there will be "nothing impure" nor anyone "who does what is shameful or deceitful" (Revelation 21:27 NIV).

We who have followed Jesus in this life, imperfectly but with a true desire, will be fully "transformed into his image" (2 Corinthians 3:18 NIV) and sealed forever. And then "'there will be no more death' or mourning or crying or pain, for the old order of things has passed away" (Revelation 21:4 NIV). That is a reward far exceeding any trials we face in this life.

Pray:

Please keep me faithful, Lord, eagerly anticipating Your rewards in eternity.

JESUS AWAITS

READ ACTS 7:51–60

Key Verse:

And he told them, "Look, I see the heavens opened and the Son of Man standing in the place of honor at God's right hand!"
ACTS 7:56 NLT

Understand:

- When you think of eternity, what things come to mind?
- Who do you want to see—again or for the very first time—when you arrive in heaven?

Apply:

One of the great promises of heaven is that this world isn't everything. Bad times on earth will be completely forgotten; even our best experiences here will be far superseded by what we find in eternity.

Consider the people you'll see there—perhaps members of your own family who've gone before, friends and coworkers and fellow church members, famous Christians of history, and even people you've read about in scripture. But the most important person, by far, will be Jesus Himself, who makes possible all of these interactions in a perfect place.

Christianity's first martyr, Stephen, was given a miraculous glimpse into heaven as he was being stoned to death. He didn't notice Moses or David or Daniel or his own mother or father. Stephen didn't exult over streets of gold or gates of pearl. He didn't even exclaim how much better heaven looks than earth. He focused exclusively on Jesus: "Look, I see the heavens opened and the Son of Man standing in the place of honor at God's right hand!" Then, as Stephen's life slipped away, he consciously placed it in Jesus' care: "Lord Jesus, receive my spirit" (verse 59 NLT).

Jesus is the focus of the entire Bible. . .and of the entire universe. He made all things (Colossians 1:16) and provides them for our pleasure (1 Timothy 6:17). But our greatest pleasure should always be in Jesus Himself.

Pray:

Lord Jesus, I'm glad You await me in heaven. Increase my love for You and help me to live in ways that honor Your greatness.

JESUS IS PREPARING A PLACE FOR YOU

READ JOHN 14:1–10

Key Verses:

"My Father's house has many rooms;
if that were not so, would I have told you
that I am going there to prepare a place for
you? And if I go and prepare a place for you,
I will come back and take you to be with
me that you also may be where I am."
JOHN 14:2–3 NIV

Understand:

- What do you think of the fact that Jesus is working on your behalf right now?
- According to this passage, what is the current benefit of the future place Jesus is preparing?

Apply:

Countless Sunday school kids have memorized John 14:2–3, and for good reason: The idea of Jesus Himself preparing a place in His Father's house *for us* is compelling. He wasn't satisfied with simply living as a man on earth, dying on the cross, coming back to life, and ascending to His heavenly home. He also wanted to make a special place for all who would follow Him.

We haven't seen heaven yet. But Jesus said, "You know the way to the place where I am going" (John 14:4 NIV). Modern Christians see the way more clearly since the completed Word of God explains what the disciple Thomas struggled to understand (verse 5). It's not a physical pathway to walk but a belief to hold on to—that Jesus is "the way and the truth and the life," and that "no one comes to the Father except through [him]" (verse 6 NIV).

Another verse worth memorizing: "Do not let your hearts be troubled. You believe in God; believe also in me" (verse 1 NIV). Knowing that Jesus is actually God, one with the Father (John 14:9–10), we can have total confidence in our future state—which provides peace today.

Pray:

Thank You, Jesus, for preparing a place for me and showing me the way. Come quickly, I pray.

A FINAL TRUTH ABOUT HEAVEN

READ PSALM 16:1–11

Key Verse:

You make known to me the path of life;
you will fill me with joy in your presence,
with eternal pleasures at your right hand.
PSALM 16:11 NIV

Understand:

- According to this psalm, what are the benefits of knowing and loving God?
- Which parts of this psalm apply to David, the writer? Which apply to the future Messiah, Jesus?

Apply:

Along with five other psalms (56–60), Psalm 16 is identified as a *miktam* of David. The meaning of the Hebrew term is unclear, though some speculate it can mean "golden" (highlighting the psalm's value) or "engraving" (indicating the psalm should be captured permanently on rock or metal). Whatever the case, Psalm 16 is certainly a valuable song that's stood the test of time.

David, the "sweet psalmist of Israel" (2 Samuel 23:1 SKJV), wrote that God was his refuge (Psalm 16:1), his only source of goodness (verse 2), his portion and cup who made his lot secure (verse 5). God would keep David steady (verse 8) and secure (verse 9) and provide a delightful inheritance (verse 6).

In Psalm 16:10, we seem to meet another character. Where David writes, "You will not abandon me to the realm of the dead, nor will you let your faithful one see decay," the text implies the coming Jewish Messiah—the descendant of David named Jesus. The apostle Peter confirmed that in his Pentecost sermon, attaching this psalm to Jesus and saying, "I can tell you confidently that the patriarch David died and was buried, and his tomb is here to this day" (Acts 2:29 NIV). But both David and Jesus could claim the promise of today's scripture—to be filled with joy in God's presence and to experience eternal pleasures at God's right hand.

This promise is ours to claim as well.

Pray:

Thank You, Jesus, for making heaven—and its eternal pleasures—available to me.

ABOUT THE AUTHOR

Paul Kent is a longtime editor who has also written several books including *Know Your Bible*, *Oswald Chambers: A Life in Pictures*, and *Playing with Purpose: Baseball Devotions*. He and his family live in Ohio's Amish Country.